Voice of the Poor

Voice of the Poor

Citizen Participation for Rebuilding New Orleans

Peter W. Dangerfield, Jr.
James Kelley Terry
Judith Williams

iUniverse, Inc.
New York Lincoln Shanghai

Voice of the Poor
Citizen Participation for Rebuilding New Orleans

iUniverse books may be ordered through booksellers or by contacting:

iUniverse
2021 Pine Lake Road, Suite 100
Lincoln, NE 68512
www.iuniverse.com
1-800-Authors (1-800-288-4677)

ISBN-13: 978-0-595-40064-5 (pbk)
ISBN-13: 978-0-595-84447-0 (ebk)
ISBN-10: 0-595-40064-7 (pbk)
ISBN-10: 0-595-84447-2 (ebk)

Printed in the United States of America

CONTENTS

PREFACE

As the citizens of New Orleans prepared for Hurricane Katrina, none expected being away from home for more than three days. Those who evacuated packed a couple of changes of clothes. Those who stayed stocked up on bottled water and batteries. Many New Orleanians who survived Hurricane Betsy made sure there was an axe in the attic, a New Orleans tradition among low-income families living east of the Industrial Canal. No one was prepared for the level of devastation that resulted from the storm and the levee failure. No one was prepared to have the realities of poverty that have characterized the Crescent City displayed so starkly before the eyes of the nation and the world. More importantly, no one was prepared for the aftermath to last so long; no one thought that six months after the storm, the city of New Orleans would be involved in one of the most massive rebuilding efforts in the history of the country.

While this project uses input from all people affected by Hurricane Katrina, particularly the largest group—low-income citizens—to develop a strategy and a policy for cleaning up and rebuilding New Orleans, it is also significant for understanding the merit of citizen participation (CP) in developing public governance. It can, in fact, be the start of a new era in New Orleans where citizens from all income levels are involved in planning, designing, implementing, monitoring, evaluating, and adjusting public governance.

In particular, this book reports on a survey conducted by Total Community Action, Inc., (TCA) in December 2005 of 708 low-income evacuees of New Orleans—one of thirty-one methods used to conduct CP efforts—in order to provide findings to elected officials, citizens, faith-based institutions, and committees and commissions set up to develop initiatives and policies for cleaning up and rebuilding New Orleans. The report also includes an account of the origin of CP, benefits and challenges to CP efforts, coupled with observations on how these benefits and challenges relate to ongoing efforts to clean up and rebuild New Orleans. Ultimately, the document seeks to help ensure that the views of low-income citizens are used to develop initiatives and formulate policies on cleaning up and rebuilding New Orleans.

WHAT IS CITIZEN PARTICIPATION

Faced with a great and serious obligation, public officials representing New Orleans have a serious responsibility to help a great but shattered city not just to recover, but also to rebuild and to become more sustainable, more equitable, and more prosperous all at once.[1] To date, the efforts to devise such a plan have included ascertaining information from civic groups, the business sector, think tanks, appointed commissions, town hall meetings, and plans produced by staff and contract services, and also include complying with state and federal directives and laws. These efforts are needed and do yield considerable, actionable, and informed direction that is invaluable when devising a plan for rebuilding New Orleans. Ironically, however, these efforts have not adequately involved citizens who live below the poverty level, who were disproportionately affected by Hurricane Katrina.

Just days before the storm, the city of New Orleans had completed the annual state of the workforce report with some positive findings. Data on poverty illustrated that New Orleans had gains in most major indicators. The Bureau of Economic Analysis reported that in 2003, New Orleans had a per capita personal income of $30,152, which was higher than the state average of $26,312 and achieved 96 percent of the national average of $31,472. Total personal income for New Orleans, which factors net earnings, dividends, interest, rent, and personal current transfer receipts, was over $14 million, an increase of 3.5 percent over 2002 figures. This figure also outperformed both the state and the nation that experienced total personal income growth of 3.3 percent and 3.2 percent, respectively. The data also revealed increases in owner-occupied housing, up to 51 percent from the 1999 figure of 46.5. However, as the challenges of accessing Federal Emergency Management Agency assistance become more public, it is becoming clear that many of New Orleans' owner-occupied housing units housed more than one family.

---

1. Brookings Institution Metropolitan Policy Program titled *New Orleans After the Storm: Lessons from the Past, a Plan for the Future*, October 2005.

However, the recently released *Chronic Poverty in New Orleans: "Pro Bono Publico" Revisited*[2] illustrates that while New Orleans and the region had shown increases in the indicators cited above, particularly in the pace of increases in per capita income, the benefits of economic growth did not accrue to all its citizens.

Chronic Poverty in New Orleans documents that in certain neighborhoods in New Orleans, the percentage of families with annual incomes of less than $30,000 was double the percentage of the city as a whole. Unemployment in these communities was significantly higher than in the rest of the city, with an overall unemployment rate of 14.8 percent. Compellingly, in these neighborhoods that were characterized by low income and high unemployment, 50 percent of all working-age persons were not actively seeking work. Moreover, for males, and particularly African-American males, in these neighborhoods, the unemployment rate was estimated to be an astounding 32 percent. For out-of-school youth age sixteen to nineteen, the picture was even more dismal, with almost 40 percent unemployment.

Noting a population decline in the areas of chronic poverty, the report suggests that the contraction of housing and the physical environments that discourage redevelopment, investment, and job creation are factors in the economic stagnation that has plagued these communities and the families they house for the past thirty years.

The catastrophic destruction caused by Hurricane Katrina includes the flooding of nearly 228,000 occupied housing units, representing more than 45 percent of the metropolitan total. This total included 120,000 owner-occupied units and 108,000 units occupied by renters, representing 39 percent and 56 percent of the respective stocks. Additionally, 38 percent of the metropolitan area's 49 extreme poverty census tracts were flooded. Moreover, *all* of the extreme poverty tracts that were flooded were located within the city of New Orleans. Clearly, while suburban growth and decentralization provided the space for the growth of black middle-class neighborhoods, the expansion of the city's footprint occurred on newly reclaimed marshland. This left these citizens with little protection, and, in many cases, it further isolated poor residents in areas east of the Industrial Canal.

These facts demonstrate, among other things, that citizens whose incomes are below the poverty line have a major stake in the rebuilding efforts. Thus, as major stakeholders and as a part of the population that knew firsthand the problem areas in New Orleans before Hurricane Katrina, their perceptions are

2.   *Chronic Poverty in New Orleans: "Pro Bono Publico" Revisited,* William H. Oakland, PhD, Peter W. Dangerfield Jr., DPA, J. Kelley Terry, 2005.

invaluable to help rebuild a shattered metropolis in a way that makes it more sustainable, more inclusive, and more economically competitive than it was before the flood. Likewise, TCA feels it is manifestly unreasonable for officials of New Orleans to rebuild without such inclusion.

In addition, history and tradition have taught that inclusive involvement in the planning of governance is considered a natural by-product of today's democracy, as well as an affirmative activity. It has allies in some basic democratic values, such as the development of citizens' individual rights and the self-actualization notions seeded by Jean-Jacques Rousseau (Pateman, 1970). It affords a process to arrive at a particular solution for those citizens, particularly on the local level, who are interested in individual and community self-determination. As such, inclusive involvement is congruent with the democratic notion that popular sovereignty is best achieved through participatory democracy. It is, therefore, appropriate that involvement is viewed as an answer to citizens' concerns about the effectiveness or lack of competence in public governance or both (Jun, 1986).

Such concerns are often induced by citizens' strong views on democratic values. These views could include the belief in a pluralistic process or a notion of building good citizens by getting them actively involved in public matters affecting their lives. Interestingly, some of these same positions on democratic values that motivate citizens to embrace involvement also have caused public administrators to examine the promise of involvement. These examinations have helped to cause a paradigm shift that has resulted in legislated involvement at all levels. As two observers write, "In philosophical terms, the realities of today's democracy are matched to the credos of the past, the needs of the present, and the options for the future" (Cahn & Passett, 1970). One effect of the trend referenced above is that it has transformed the work of public administrators and public managers (Thomas, 1995). TCA hopes that the events of August 29, 2005, bring public administrators and leadership in New Orleans closer to this position because of the benefits to the rebuilding process and the sound public management that is a natural outcome of citizen participation—and that is long overdue.

Moreover, CP could help in the rebuilding process by introducing systems thinking. This tenet has been observed as far back as the writings of Aristotle, who is considered to be a founder of citizen involvement. An example is evidenced in Aristotle's use of the analogy of the "policy shoe" (Murray & Price, 1996), in which he pointed out that the citizen wearing the shoe is better able to tell where it pinches than the maker of the shoe. Arguably, the poor, particularly the working poor, should be able to objectively talk about the pinches that affected them, with emphasis on post-Katrina effects. Aristotle believed that there is strength and wisdom in numbers, compared with one policy-maker or participant. It was argued that collective wisdom could offset the narrow perspective of one or a few participants.

The logic of systems thinking is that involvement is a prerequisite for the continued survival and improvement of a political system. Here, the view is that the planning process used in New Orleans has not historically responded to the demands arising from the disadvantaged of the city unless mandated as a condition of funding. This has resulted in less-effective governance.

Because of the importance of input from the largest and most affected group, coupled with the fact that the poor are often underrepresented in planning, decision-making, and policy-making processes, as well as the historical, the traditional, and the practical value placed on involvement of affected citizens, TCA conducted a literature review and prospectus of CP. They also constructed and administered a CP survey to ascertain input from the displaced, disadvantaged citizens of New Orleans on their perceptions of ways to rebuild New Orleans. Derivatively, it is TCA's hope that the findings of both will be given weight and considered in tandem with input from other groups and will also be decisively used to inform and set policy for rebuilding New Orleans. This report starts with foundational notes on CP.

Definition of and Tools for Accomplishing Citizen Participation

Until the creation of the Committee for a Better New Orleans, there was no formal or organized and sustained effort to implement citizen participation in public governance. As the committee learned, agreeing on a definition of CP and defining the tools and/or processes used to collect input are challenging. This section defines both.

Viewpoints on the definition of CP are diverse. Pateman (1970) notes that the term "participation" refers to a wide variety of different situations by various authors. Clark (2000) attributes this to the fact that designers of modern-day CP did not discuss the concept of CP in detail before incorporating it into the antipoverty legislation in the 1960s. Rather, individuals interested in CP were left to their own devices in defining the concept. The intent was to afford disadvantaged citizens maximum feasible participation in planning, execution, and evaluation in governance affecting their lives. Before the maximum feasible participation intervention, citizens participated in government by electing persons to represent them in organizations, as well as in both the judicial and legislative branches (Cooper, 1982). The result of CP, Thomas (1995) suggests, is that participation has been broadened to include the direct involvement of citizens in both policy formation and implementation. Thus, for the purposes of this project, TCA is defining CP as maximum feasible involvement of disadvantaged citizens in the formulation of plans for cleaning up and rebuilding New Orleans through the incorporation of the findings of their views along with the views of other affected groups from New Orleans.

Mechanisms for CP are defined as the tools and/or processes used in the collection of data on the opinions, preferences, needs, desires, and expectations of citizens for the purpose of informing policy-and decision-making.

Arnstein and Metcalf (1976) and Thomas (1995) identified and described a number of mechanisms of CP. Arnstein and Metcalf provide a list of thirty-seven CP mechanisms, and Thomas provides a list of eleven. Of the mechanisms in Thomas' list, six have been extensively used, while the mechanisms reported by Arnstein include some experimental mechanisms and some mechanisms that have been designed but not field-tested. Ten of the mechanisms identified by Arnstein and Metcalf and Thomas have been tried in the field, either singularly or in combination, as concluded by the authors.

Thomas' (1995) mechanisms for attaining citizen input are based on the extent to which the public should be involved. The options, according to the author, are to involve the public in obtaining information only or to involve the public for both input and acceptance, while offering influence in exchange. Assuming the former, he offers four mechanisms: (1) new communication technologies, (2) citizen—initiated contacts with agencies, (3) key contacts, and (4) citizen surveys. Of these mechanisms, current and past administrators in New Orleans have used some form of key contact as a CP mechanism, i.e., the engagement of key businesspersons, accomplished and highly visible officials of faith-based institutions, universities, one or two community activists, etc., for their input. Though well intentioned, this practice is a far cry from Thomas' view of key contact.

For officials in New Orleans interested in obtaining information from citizens in a manner that produces citizen buy-in of the decision or policy, Thomas (1995) offers seven mechanisms: (1) volunteerism, (2) ombudsperson, (3) action centers, (4) institutionalized citizens' roles in decision making, (5) public meetings, (6) advisory committees, and (7) mediation/arbitration. Of these mechanisms, Thomas advises that public meetings, advisory committees, and negotiation and mediation are the most widely used mechanisms for achieving this end. Here again, past and current administrators have used both public meetings and advisory committees and, as with key contacts, have fallen short of the intended outcome of building policy based on the input of citizens.

From Arnstein and Metcalf's (1976) list, the mechanisms for direct CP that have been tested in the field include advisory committees, advocacy planning, citizens' representatives on public policy-making bodies, public and community meetings and hearings, community planning and drop-in centers, community technical assistance, and ombudspersons. Also, focus group discussions and surveys are provided by Arnstein and Metcalf as the mechanisms of indirect CP that have the most field use and popularity among public managers and policy-makers. Like Thomas, Arnstein and Metcalf (1976) also identify communications technology-based mechanisms, such as computer-based techniques, citizens' hotlines, interactive cable TV-based participation, and media-based balloting. However, the writers conclude that these mechanisms have been implemented by only a few organizations. Additionally, Arnstein and Metcalf offer specific methods for planning, organizing, and analyzing (i.e., "fishbowl" planning, group dynamics, plural planning, value analysis, Delphi method, relative weighting, etc.). Here again, the literature search indicates that these methods are seldom used by organizations. Also, by definition, these methods are specific techniques that are incorporated in public and group meeting mechanisms of CP.

Another mechanism of CP that has seldom been tried, and yet shows promise, is action research (Cooper & Musso, 1999). Action research functions similarly to an action center, it enables citizens and community groups to plan through continuous availability of multidisciplinary professionals. Although intended to facilitate the development of neighborhood organizations, the concept, arguably, has promise for building the intellectual capacity of existing neighborhood organizations, thus enhancing the organization's chances of being co-producers. Utilizing action research, the potential for co-production is improved because neighborhood organizations can obtain technical assistance from a university, making them less dependent on government experts.

More often than not, these mechanisms cannot be applied without some adjustments that support the conditions of a local area. For example, there is a major sense of urgency to repopulate New Orleans. Hence, time and resources needed for a full-blown CP effort are neither advisable nor practical. Developing initiatives and formulating policies to repopulate New Orleans without CP—in particular, input from low-income people—is also neither advisable nor practical. Moreover, repopulation data suggests that over 300,000 New Orleans residents remain in the Diaspora, and, as such, maximum participation must be a factor both in the capacity and in the feasibility of accessing the displaced population. Accordingly, with some adaptation, the lists that follow identify CP approaches that the city of New Orleans can use to achieve CP, given the realities regarding the post-Katrina citizenship of the city.

Direct Participation Mechanisms

- Ombudsperson: an independent, impartial administrative officer who serves as mediator between the citizens and the government or agency for the redress of citizen complaints and grievances
- Action centers: a mechanism that enables citizens and community groups to plan through the continuous availability of multidisciplinary professional and technical assistance
- Institutionalized citizens' roles: representative membership on public boards
- Public/community meetings and hearings: open, advertised meetings for discussion of issues and policy
- Key contacts: engagement of key members of the community (i.e., grassroots community leaders, community advocates, businesspersons, leaders of faith-based institutions, think tanks, special committees, labor leaders, etc.)
- Advisory committees: a group of citizens called together or appointed by an agency to provide advice and consultation to the agency on behalf of the citizens of their community
- Mediation/arbitration: utilization of an independent party to resolve issues and disputes that arise between policy-and decision-making agencies and citizens (Mediation/arbitration is considered a CP mechanism in those instances in which a public policy or decision is made without a CP process and lacks the buy-in and support of the citizenry.)

Indirect Participation Mechanisms

- Citizen surveys: use of questionnaires to solicit opinions, input, and feedback
- Focus group discussions: group interviews designed to obtain feedback and to measure reactions

Notably, volunteerism, citizen-initiated contacts, and advocacy planning are not included in the final list of mechanisms, as each requires initiation by the individual citizen and, as such, does not meet the definition of mechanisms of CP as actionable from the perspective of the public manager or policy-maker.

CHALLENGE TO USING FINDINGS/INPUT TO DEVELOP INITIATIVES AND POLICIES (NEW ORLEANS)

In order to understand the challenges in implementing initiatives and policies based, in part, on CP, one must first understand factors affecting CP implementation. For example, it is instructive to know that factors affecting the implementation of CP are political, social, and organizational conditions and actions or roles that are designed to facilitate, enhance, hinder, impede, or delay a CP effort. Further, these factors have the potential to maximize or limit the type and amount of citizen involvement. Defined in this manner, factors that are designed to facilitate the implementation of CP can either positively or negatively impact CP and are generally known or planned for prior to implementation. These factors include strategies for implementation, responsibility for implementation, methods and processes of communication and outreach, and funding mechanisms for the CP effort. Finally, the literature further identifies certain conditions that can occur during a CP process that must be strategically managed in order to maximize a CP effort.

These factors would be relevant in any CP initiative, notwithstanding the current state of planning, rebuilding, and redeveloping with which New Orleans is faced. Compellingly, the devastation caused by Katrina, the levee failures, and the continued displacement of over 300,000 residents in general—and low-income residents in particular—makes attention to the factors that enhance or impede CP both more critical to the process and more meaningful to the outcomes.

Among the strategies for implementation identified in the literature is that of building the capacity of citizens to effectively participate in the process. Kaufmann (1991), for example, proposed the notion that participating in a public process entails interorganizational bargaining, which, in order to be effective, requires procedural knowledge, negotiation skills, organizational competencies, power (not defined by Kaufman), and money to articulate and accomplish one's claim collectively. Assuming that the position of Kaufman is correct, it is arguable that strategies to maximize CP would involve efforts to ensure that citizens, particularly low-income citizens, are provided with the assistance and/or resources that build their capacity to successfully participate.

Building on Kaufmann's (1991) approach, Box (1998) suggests the utilization of information on political, social, economic, and other major factors that shape the dynamics of local areas as a starting point for developing a CP process. More specifically, Box counsels that these factors represent decision points (i.e., is the political power structure open or closed to citizens; what alliances exist within the community; do economic and social conditions limit the availability of resources, etc.) that should be considered prior to implementing CP. Box's advice is sound and commonsensical, and his observations about this and other features in his proposal are that they are situation specific. That is, CP efforts must be designed and planned in a manner that fits the contextual boundaries of the community and represents the political, social, and economic values of the citizenry.

Berry, Portney, and Thomson (1993) counsel implementers of a CP effort to consider the role of socioeconomic status (SES), race, and ethnicity in the CP process. Noting what they observe as a strong correlation between political participation and these factors, they argue that it is advisable for a public manager to factor participation from various groups in the CP approach. They state:

> Previous studies have established a clear linkage between SES and political participation, finding that political participants are disproportionately likely to be of higher income and socioeconomic status. This relationship is often referred to as the "standard socioeconomic model" of participation. (p. 81)

To demonstrate this point, the writers use findings from the cities their study covers, showing that CP levels in low SES areas are considerably lower than in the middle, above-average, and high SES areas. By extension, this researcher asserts that factoring SES into a model for CP, and thereby ensuring that the participation of citizens is representative of the community of interest, should afford a means for broadening the focus of the CP effort to be representative of the community at large. This is particularly relevant to New Orleans because it consists of a significant number of low-income citizens. Thus, unless specific efforts are made in the planning stage for inclusion of all citizens, particularly low-income, their views are not considered similar to those of other stakeholders in New Orleans.

Similarly, another factor influencing the implementation of CP is the extent to which there can be a sophisticated political balance in which citizens, governments, or advocates rise above partisan politics (Berry et al., 1993). The necessary precursor, Berry et al. agree, is finding a means to balance business and resident interests. Also, those organizations participating in the CP process, the writers further assert, must have open membership that is available to people of all political parties and persuasions. Additionally, these organizations as a group must not take a stand on political candidates. Admittedly, politics is always present. Nevertheless, TCA contends that partisan politics should be managed to the extent that it is not a dominant driver. Rather, nonpartisan politics, like other considerations, becomes part and parcel of an organization's CP process. Thomson, Berry, and Portney (1994) contend that the political organization of citizens around specific neighborhood issues can be accomplished without candidate or partisan considerations toward a stable political balance that supports effective CP. Even though this judgment opens up the writers to dispute, they sufficiently make the point that partisan politics has the potential to limit the amount and type of citizen involvement by limiting access to the members of a particular political party (group) and/or limiting the agenda and policy options to those favored by a particular political party. As such, political balance is a factor affecting the implementation of CP.

In the last twenty-five years, there has not been a formal effort in New Orleans to balance the interests of businesses and residents, i.e., an effort where elected officials institute an ongoing process for ascertaining the views and interests of residents and businesses and using both to set governance. Rather, what exists is a tradition in which various committees are formed, consisting mainly of businesspersons, representation from well-organized neighborhoods, and faith-based and special interest groups with limited representation from citizens at large. Derivatively, policies evolving from this process are not a balance of businesses and residents but a balance of businesses and well-organized groups.

Another issue that influences the implementation of CP is the interest and motivation of citizens to be involved and make things work (Berry et al., 1993; Pateman, 1970). This interest is both seeded and fueled by citizens who feel that their involvement in public efforts can have a significant impact on final policy/decisions. As such, the political environment must allow citizens to have this level of impact (Berry et al., 1993). Additionally, these authors note that citizen interest is similarly dependent upon the feeling that their involvement is enabled and actively protected by federal law, and they advise that the participation process must be related to a specific government policy or program decision. As such, given the dependence of citizens on government to protect the CP process and ultimately to implement the outcomes, the role of public managers in the implementation of CP is a factor that needs to be addressed.

Based on empirical analysis, Thomas (1995), Berry et al. (1993), and Cooper and Musso (1999) make the suggestion that CP is effective if the environment affords a systematic flow of information to neighborhoods and support for neighborhood outreach and communication. In essence, the political and administrative environment must possess a process or communications structure that ensures equal access to neighborhood citizens and provides realistic opportunities for a large number of citizens of a target area to participate. Focusing directly on the neighborhood level, Cooper and Musso make the case that the administrative environment must afford formal identification and recognition of neighborhood organizations and that the political environment must include a structure or process that allows mediation between neighborhood organizations and elected officials (Kraut & Kraut, 1985).

Government funding of the CP effort is an influential factor affecting implementation. Berry et al., (1993) weigh in on this point by asserting that it is perhaps the most important reason that participation has worked, while Thomas (1995) asserts that the results of this consideration are mixed. Berry et al. show that, with the exception of San Antonio, cities having CP initiatives instituted them with financial assistance from local governments, doing so before the cities became financially challenged or before they encountered overwhelming political reversals. Thomas, on the other hand, recognizes the need for financial assistance, yet gives a sound reason for being cautious of government funding, i.e., "subsidies compromise the ability of many organizations to advocate for their communities." Clearly, government funding is a factor affecting the implementation of CP, and the impact of government funding of CP efforts is an issue that must be explored.

Another dominant perspective holds that a CP effort should be citywide (Berry et al., 1993; Marston and Towers, 1993; Musso, 2000; Thomas, 1995). The logic is to afford every citizen the opportunity to participate in public governance.

Barriers impeding CP are also factors affecting implementation, as these conditions are generally encountered during the implementation of a CP effort. Barriers include such factors as delays in decision-making and the subsequent increase in costs, lack of support of public managers, interest group control and manipulation, government control, and micromanagement by citizens.

Cupps (1977) describes delays in decision-making as a barrier to CP. Generally, time is added to the period to finalize a project because citizens are directly involved in providing input and influencing the resulting decisions and policies. An extension of the theory is that delays in decision-making cause increased cost to be associated with getting citizens organized and involved in providing input on public policy issues and service delivery (Mikulecky, 1990).

The attitudes of public managers can also be an impediment to CP. While CP is institutionalized in public policy-making through both legislative action and political behavior, many professionals who do not sufficiently value input from citizens and do not adopt a participative style impede the implementation of CP. For CP to be effective, professionals and/or managers must cooperate with residents in order to design delivery systems that best meet the needs of a community. If not, citizens will perceive, as in the case of New Orleans during the terms of the past four administrations, resistance by professionals and managers as professional usurpation of democratic community control (Box, 1998).

Additionally, the potential for single-or special-interest groups to overwhelm CP is a barrier that must be factored into the planning and implementation of CP. Granted, all groups have legitimate rights to have their views and causes heard and considered by officials. However, the potential for the narrowly focused viewpoints and bias of single-and special-interest groups in the CP process is a factor with the potential for limiting involvement in the CP process (Iglitzin, 1995). Because this practice is so well entrenched in New Orleans, it is manifestly unreasonable to expect the balancing of interest without institution of a CP process. Similarly, Moyniham's (1969) concept of CP as a means for government control also presents a factor that impedes CP. Observers of the notion of the potential for abuse assert that either government or special interest groups can abuse CP, either through control of the agenda, or through manipulation of the process, or both.

Finally, the notion of the potential for citizens to become overly involved in operations presents an administrative impediment to CP that must be addressed in developing a CP model. Currently, there are no signs of this happening in New Orleans.

Several themes in organizational theory, such as individual participation, empowerment, and the decentralization of decision-making authority, demonstrate the best way that public entities can manage challenges, meaningfully involve citizens in the planning and operation of an organization, and derive benefits when changes are made. One dominant school of thought regarding benefits determines that responsiveness is attained through CP in which citizens see their involvement as contributing to an increased influence in public policy-making and public administrators see this involvement as a means to improve a public entity's effectiveness. For example, it is believed that CP affords public administrators a process that permits the development of more implementable polices (Box, 1998; Nunn, 2001; Plumlee, Starling and Kramer,

1985; Thomas, 1995; Whitaker, 1980) than would be developed without such a process. Equally important, these policies would be implementable because CP is grounded in democratic theory and, as such, is believed to be consistent with democratic values. An example might occur in which there is a mechanism in a public organization that effectively uses individuals' views or places value on input from citizens affected by a planned policy where broad public acceptance is achieved, the chance for efficient discharging of a public responsibility is enhanced, or both (Cole, 1981; Thomas, 1995).

Summary of CP

This study demonstrates that CP is difficult to effectively institute, while making the case that New Orleans and, by extension, the state and other affected cities will benefit from a well-planned and efficiently executed CP project that uses the input of the affected citizens to develop public governance. Second, the study shows that CP theory provides a map that elected officials and public administrators can use to chart a course for instituting a CP plan. Third, the research shows that CP theory is as old as democratic theory, and it will be around for some time. Fourth, the opportunity to participate in rebuilding efforts is critical to the development of citizenship. Thus, any mechanism that provides an additional forum for such participation would be beneficial. By extension, if New Orleans provides an opportunity for its citizens to participate in the governance structures, the potential for rebuilding New Orleans would be greatly enhanced (Levine, 1984). Fifth, of the thirty methods/tools for accomplishing CP, conducting a survey is appropriate for obtaining the views and actionable opinions from low-income people on what is needed to clean up and rebuild New Orleans. Also, given the constraints and logistics, conducting a citizen survey meets the test of inclusion of low-income citizens and access to affected populations and accomplishes both expeditiously so as to minimize planning delays and costs. Finally, CP has instructive implications for planning.

IMPLICATIONS FOR PLANNING

By and large, planners define citizen participation as any effort to collect input from community residents. Their attempts to involve citizens occur mainly to satisfy legislative requirements for federal and state funding. Local planners have less time for public participation because they have to reduce delays in plan preparation. Thus, CP has become trivialized as simply a step in the planning process that must be completed to comply with federal and state regulations.

By derivation, one of the greatest challenges to planners is to set up local mechanisms that allow for authentic participation and bring true influence to bear on policy formulations. Such activities could shift the responsibility for improving or changing neighborhood conditions to the residents and could function to enhance their sense of empowerment and, ultimately, their sense of community. Thus, the primary implication for planning practice raises the question of what role planners are willing to adopt to facilitate CP. A constructive role would require planners to organize, inform, and instill confidence in the local citizenry. Planners should bring about situations in which local citizens demand power and actively seek control over decisions that affect their lives. Moreover, citizens should be able to participate in the design of the process rather than the process being constructed without them, while the citizens are simply expected to conform to something they had no input in creating. Rauhe and Lyons (2000) states:

> The key to this approach, however, lies not in the "who," the "what," or the "where," but the "how." Planners have long played the role of expert advisers. A lesser number immerse themselves in the local political process, but this is hardly revolutionary. Yet, all too rare are the instances where planners have systematically attempted to educate at every opportunity rather than jealously guard their knowledge; to patiently permit stakeholders to work through their own political problems, even facilitating that process, rather than attempting to control it or avoid it altogether; and to place the responsibility for planning, implementation, and evaluation on local stakeholders rather than gathering input and going off to do the "real work" them-

14

selves. These latter process elements constitute true empowerment and lasting change in local planning and development.

Finally, the planning implication for CP means readiness of both the local government and citizens to accept certain responsibilities and activities. It should also mean that the value of each group's contribution is seen, appreciated, and used in the planning process. Therefore, it is necessary for the people to be involved in all stages of planning, design, implementation, and evaluation. To improve public participation in the planning system, there has to be a more distinctive connection between participation and decision-making. This means reestablishing bonds of trust between the public and political institutions. To ensure secure trust, planners involved in the CP process must ensure that the involvement by all parties is transparent.

All factors considered, a survey is the best tool for ascertaining the views of dislocated, disadvantaged residents of New Orleans. The survey comports with the normative perspective where elected officials and leaders can (1) meet new challenges, such as responsiveness and inclusion of the poor; (2) reach out to the poor as stakeholders; and (3) incorporate their input and preferences, within reason, into the policy recommendations. The model is incremental at best (Lindblom, 1959). Nevertheless, it is more than a minimal departure from the status quo, and the poor are viewed as stakeholders with a formal means of affecting decisions and/or policies on rebuilding. Furthermore, the model is congruent with the tenets of participatory democracy (Berry et al., 1993; Box, 1998; Weeks, 2000) and the emerging management practices of using customer/citizen input in decision-and policy-making (Crosby, Kelly and Schaefer, 1986; Galbraith and Lawler, 1993), particularly where citizens are viewed as co-producers of decisions (Whitaker, 1980) in the operations/services (Robertson, 1995; Thomas, 1995) that are provided by a community-based organization. The survey model is also congruent with Cooper and Musso's (1999) observation that a public involvement process should be tailored to respond to the cultural conditions. There is an abundance of interdisciplinary support that shows that poor citizens are a major part of the culture of New Orleans. Thus, the remainder of this book details the methodology that was used to conduct the CP survey, findings, and observations on actionable steps that officials can take in the cleanup and rebuilding efforts.

METHODOLOGY FOR CONDUCTING THE SURVEY

Sampling low-income evacuees across the United States is considered difficult because this is a hidden population and there is no appropriate sampling frame. Several methods to achieve some form of random selection were reviewed by researchers of this survey. One of these is a snowball sampling. The central concept is locating new respondents through introductions from initial contact persons.

Essentially, three phases make up the snowballing method. First, there is network mapping and referral procedure in which respondents are randomly selected and asked to refer another respondent until the process is completed. The second phase is interviewing. After random selection, people are contacted and interviewed. Third is the repeating procedure phase. Here, every group of nominees represents a stage. A line of respondent-referral-respondent-referral through the stages forms the snowball chain. A chain stops when no more nominations can be given or when the selected individual is not found or refuses to participate. In this way, several chains can be created throughout a population.

The interviews are preceded by site sampling, a selection procedure in which the evacuee population is divided with regard to geographic location (cities where evacuees are located) and the time (when evacuees are at the selected locations).

Randomization is achieved by making a random choice out of a set of possible respondents (evacuees), as opposed to asking every evacuee that is located by snowballing. At the zero stage, respondents are selected randomly at the sites chosen for sampling. The individuals who are selected to respond are again asked to nominate other evacuees to participate. By repeating this procedure, evacuees from sample sites are interviewed.

This sampling technique has been used in some major sociological studies of working-class and poor households in the United States and has received widespread acclaim for its contributions to the field. In turn, research methodologists have pointed to the advantages of snowball sampling, not only for providing greater efficiency, but also for enabling a better understanding of individuals and individual households within their social context. That is, random samples tend to focus on isolated individuals or households. In contrast, snowball sampling allows the researcher to identify networks of social relationships between these individuals and households. Moreover, such networks of social interaction have been documented in other sociological studies as providing important networks of social support, particularly in poor communities.

With respect to sample size, because there is no list for random selection to ensure equal probability, TCA believes a minimum of 700 New Orleans dislocated residents interviewed in twenty cities is reasonable. An explanation for this decision follows.

Based on official reports and accounts from the media and other informed sources, evacuees relocated primarily to twenty cities—Houston-Baytown-Sugar Land, TX; New Orleans-Metairie-Kenner, LA; Baton Rouge, LA; Beaumont-Port Arthur, TX; Mobile, AL; Gulfport-Biloxi, MS; Jackson, MS; Houma-Bayou Cane-Thibodaux, LA; Lake Charles, LA; Dallas-Fort Worth-Arlington, TX; Pascagoula, MS; Hattiesburg, MS; Lafayette, LA; Atlanta-Sandy Springs-Marietta, GA; Shreveport-Bossier City, LA; Austin-Round Rock, TX; Alexandria, LA; San Antonio, TX; Memphis, TN-MS-AR; and Los Angeles-Long Beach-Santa Ana, CA (**see Figure 1**).

Table 1

Reported Locations of Katrina/Rita Applicants from Louisiana, Mississippi, Alabama, and Texas Disasters as of October 31, 2005

This list reflects the applicants' reporting of their locations, including those who have evacuated outside of the hurricane-impacted areas. It is as current as any subsequent change of address notifications they have given to FEMA. There are approximately 600,000 additional applicants who gave current addresses outside of U.S. Census Metropolitan Statistical Areas.

Ranking	CBSA	Metropolitan Statistical Area Name	*State	Number of Applicants
1	26420	Houston-Baytown-Sugar Land, TX	TX	304,232
2	35380	New Orleans-Metairie-Kenner, LA	LA	281,006
3	12940	Baton Rouge, LA	LA	202,042
4	13140	Beaumont-Port Arthur, TX	TX	110,922
5	33660	Mobile, AL	AL	89,059
6	25060	Gulfport-Biloxi, MS	MS	88,646
7	27140	Jackson, MS	MS	80,255
8	26380	Houma-Bayou Cane-Thibodaux, LA	LA	66,854
9	29340	Lake Charles, LA	LA	61,260
10	19100	Dallas-Fort Worth-Arlington, TX	TX	59,617
11	37700	Pascagoula, MS	MS	58,490
12	25620	Hattiesburg, MS	MS	45,984
13	29180	Lafayette, LA	LA	43,323
14	12060	Atlanta-Sandy Springs-Marietta, GA	GA	38,279
15	43340	Shreveport-Bossier City, LA	LA	14,418
16	12420	Austin-Round Rock, TX	TX	13,544
17	10780	Alexandria, LA	LA	13,350
18	41700	San Antonio, TX	TX	13,142
19	32820	Memphis, TN-MS-AR	TN	10,652
20	31100	Los Angeles-Long Beach-Santa Ana, CA	CA	7,216

Total applicants reporting addresses in an MSA: 1,890,985

Ranking = based on the number of applicants to FEMA living in a U.S. Census Metropolitan Statistical Area (MSA)

CBSA = U.S. Census code for Metropolitan Statistical Area

*State = the first state in a multi-state Metropolitan Statistical Area

Source: FEMA's Recovery Division provided data from registration intake reports. The figures are based on the best available data.

Because these numbers on locations are available, TCA decided to include a minimum number of citizens from each of these same sites (cities) by using (1) the reported number of Katrina/Rita applicants for each city; (2) a determination of the total number of Katrina/Rita applicants for the twenty cities; and (3) the percentage of each city based on the total of twenty cities, coupled with information from official reports and media accounts on evacuees in each area to determine how many surveys to use from each city. The breakdown of the results for each city follows:

City	No. of Applicants	% of Total Applicants	Sample Size Per City
Houston-Baytown-Sugar Land, TX	304,232	19%	133
New Orleans-Metairie-Kenner, LA	281,006	18%	126
Baton Rouge, LA	202,042	13%	91
Beaumont-Port Arthur, TX	110,922	7%	49
Mobile, AL	89,059	6%	42
Gulfport-Biloxi, MS	88,646	6%	42
Jackson, MS	80,255	5%	35
Houma-Bayou Cane-Thibodaux, LA	66,854	4%	28
Lake Charles, LA	61,260	4%	21
Dallas-Fort Worth-Arlington, TX	59,617	4%	21
Pascagoula, MS	58,490	4%	21
Hattiesburg, MS	45,984	3%	21
Lafayette, LA	43,323	3%	21
Atlanta-Sandy Springs-Marietta, GA	38,279	2%	14
Shreveport-Bossier City, LA	14,418	1%	7
Austin-Round Rock, TX	13,544	1%	7
Alexandria, LA	13,350	1%	7
San Antonio, TX	13,142	1%	7
Memphis, TN-MS-AR	10,652	1%	7
Los Angeles-Long Beach-Santa Ana, CA	7,216	0%	7
TOTAL:	**1,602,291**		**707**

Based on sample size, fifteen interviewers were employed, trained, and monitored to administer surveys in Houston-Baytown-Sugar Land, TX: New Orleans-Metairie-Kenner, LA; Baton Rouge, LA; Beaumont-Port Arthur, TX; Mobile, AL; Gulfport-Biloxi, MS; Jackson, MS; Houma-Bayou Cane-Thibodaux, LA; Lake Charles, LA; Dallas-Fort Worth-Arlington, TX; Pascagoula, MS; Hattiesburg, MS; Lafayette, LA; Atlanta-Sandy Springs-Marietta, GA; Shreveport-Bossier City, LA; Austin-Round Rock, TX; Alexandria, LA; San Antonio, TX; Memphis, TN-MS-AR; and Los Angeles-Long Beach-Santa Ana, CA. Community Action Agencies operating in the remaining areas, i.e., Beaumont-Port Arthur, TX; Mobile, AL; Gulfport-Biloxi, MS; Lake Charles, LA; Pascagoula, MS; Hattiesburg, MS; San Antonio, TX; and Memphis TN-MS-AR, were asked to administer questionnaires in their areas.

GEOGRAPHICAL INFORMATION SYSTEM

Coding and analysis of the findings included demographic and spatial analysis utilizing state-of-the-art Geographic Information System (GIS) support. This level of analysis affords TCA staff and officials an opportunity to view information at the city, parish, community, neighborhood, and even block levels. Used as an overlay to census data, the resulting information presents a clear picture of the representation of low-income citizens in the survey.

Further, the analysis produces information for TCA and other agencies serving New Orleans' poor to use in developing initiatives to help citizens who are planning to return to New Orleans but who will be unable to return to their pre-Katrina residences. Finally, the combined demographic and geographic analysis supports long-term planning efforts for the type of proactive development that affords the building of mixed-income communities and the de-densification of chronically poor neighborhoods.

The geo-coding of the survey results is provided in Appendix A.

VOLUNTEER EFFORT

The survey was administered by TCA, Inc., with assistance from Outsource, Inc., a firm based in New Orleans with a strong background in GIS, CP, and conducting CP surveys. Specifically, the firm pre-tested the questionnaire, made suggested changes, coded the survey, analyzed the data and developed the findings, trained interviewers and supervisors of interviewers, provided GIS coding, and made itself available for a discussion of the findings. In return for this assistance, TCA gave Outsource all intellectual property derived from the survey, provided the property is not used in diatribes, political campaigns, unbalanced news reports, stratagem, contrivance, machination, or a disingenuous manner or to criticize a position, individual, or organization. In addition assistance was received from other Community Action agencies in the southeast United States during the survey administration period of December 2005 to February 2006.

QUESTIONNAIRE

The questions consisted of both closed-ended and open-ended precoded information. See Appendix B for a copy of the questionnaire.

SURVEY FINDINGS

In the main, the survey was designed to elicit information in five major areas: (1) the problems and challenges facing low-and moderate-income evacuees, both those who have already decided to return to New Orleans and those who are undecided; (2) the recommendations on what should be done to rebuild New Orleans to better serve the citizens; (3) the communications with and involvement of citizens in the planning and rebuilding efforts and the best methods for accomplishing each; (4) the confidence of citizens in the ability of local government to impact the conditions of poverty that character-ize New Orleans neighborhoods; and (5) the willingness of citizens to invest in rebuilding New Orleans through increased taxes. In addition to the general findings relative to each major issue area explored in the survey, the analysis also examines the differences in responses across participant categories, i.e., respondents who have made the decision to return to New Orleans, those who would like to return, those who have decided not to return, and those who remain undecided.

Problems and Challenges Facing Low-and Moderate-Income Evacuees

In understanding the impact of Hurricane Katrina on New Orleans' low-and moderate-income citizens, it is important to have a better understanding of the stability of citizens since the storm. As such, analysis of the survey responses revealed that on the average, low-and moderate-income evacuees have moved 2.32 times in the four months following Hurricane Katrina and that most (55 percent) have lived at their current addresses for three months or less, as illustrated below.

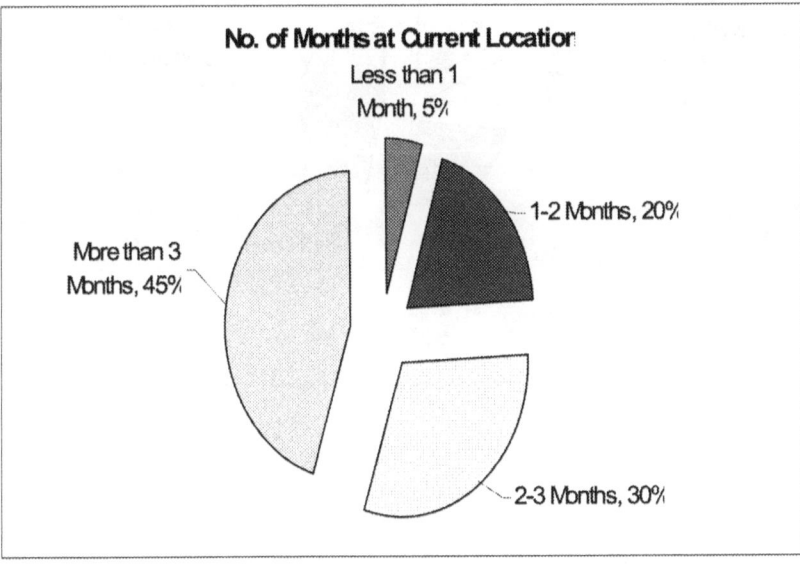

With regard to the decision of evacuees to return to New Orleans, only 46 percent responded with a definite decision to return and only 10 percent with a definite decision not to return, as illustrated below.

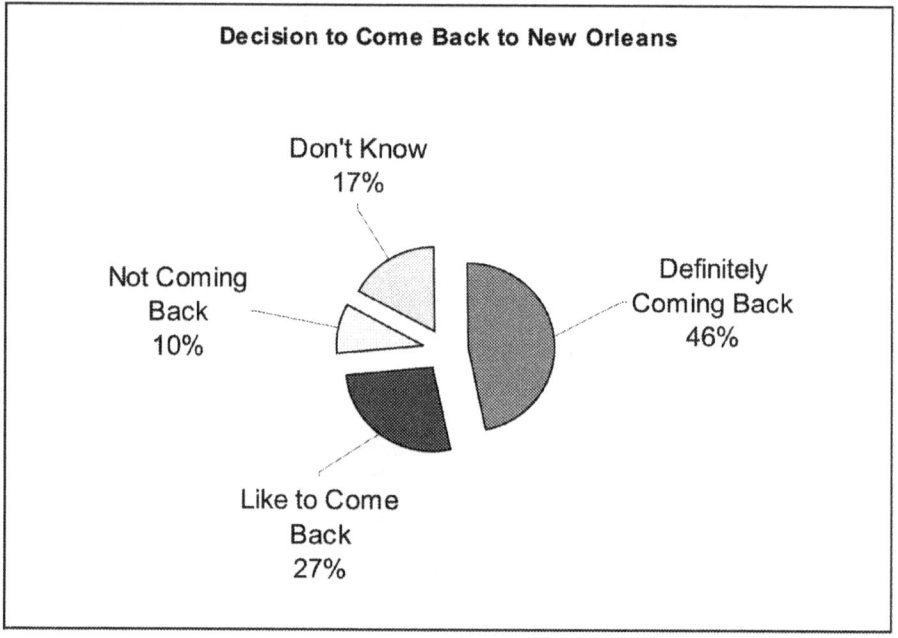

Decision to Come Back to New Orleans

Don't Know 17%

Not Coming Back 10%

Definitely Coming Back 46%

Like to Come Back 27%

Analysis of the demographic profile of each respondent group revealed some notable trends.

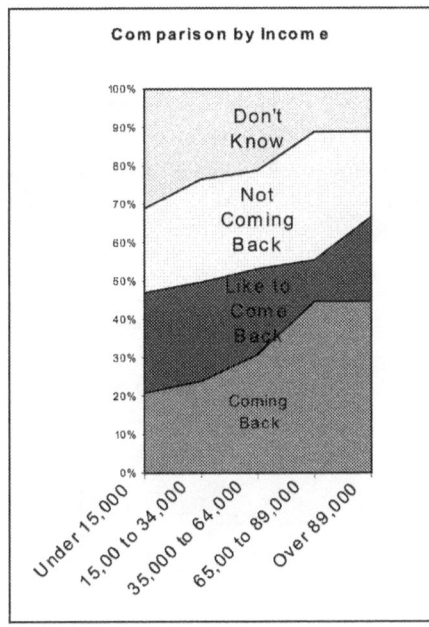
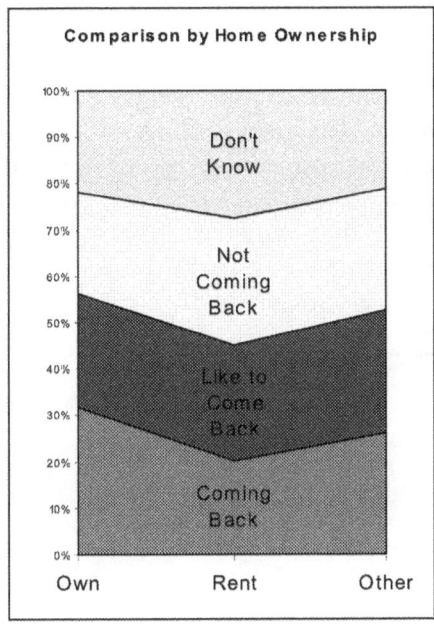

With regard to income, lower income levels (annual household income under $15,000) evidenced higher levels of uncertainty, with 42 percent undecided and 35 percent in the like to come back category with no definite decision to return or not. Additionally, a definite decision to return to New Orleans was more likely as income increased.

No clear patterns emerged relative to age or the presence of children under the age of eighteen in the household. However, relative to homeownership, it is noteworthy that of the survey respondents indicating a decision not to return to New Orleans, 33 percent were homeowners. Compellingly, of the participants indicating a definite decision not to return, over half (52 percent) were single and over one-third (36 percent) were between the ages of twenty-five and thirty-four.

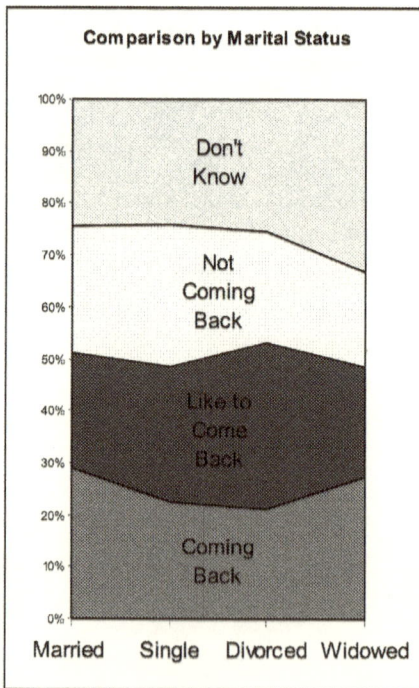

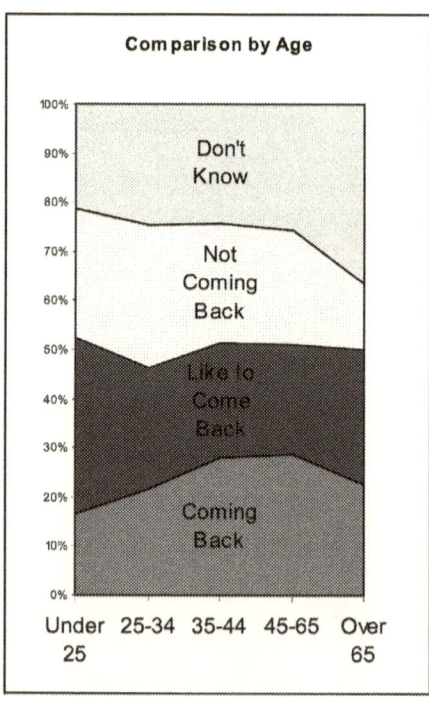

With regard to race, the one distinct pattern that emerged from the analysis was the high level of uncertainty among African American survey participants. Of the undecided participants, 84 percent were African American and 13 percent were white.

One of the most telling indicators was the finding relative to the decision to return based on employment. While higher-income residents were more likely to return, among low-to moderate-income residents, unemployed adults were more likely to return than those who were employed. Of the participants indicating a definite decision to return, 37 percent were employed and 63 percent were unemployed. Similarly, of those deciding not to return, the majority (57 percent) were employed.

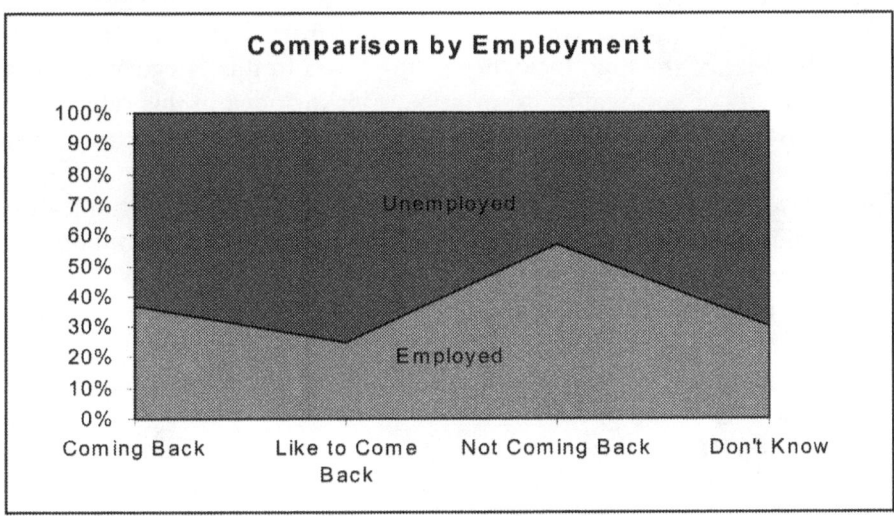

Moreover, among the survey respondents receiving public assistance, i.e., Aid to Families of Dependent Children (AFDC), Food Stamps, Medicaid, etc., the highest frequency of receipt of public assistance benefits was among participants indicating a definite decision to return to New Orleans.

No clear pattern emerged with regard to gender; however, there appears to be a slightly higher degree of uncertainty among women than among male participants.

An open-ended question was used in identifying the most important problems facing citizens who evacuated New Orleans, with seven distinct response themes ranging from housing and relocation to emotional and social issues, as detailed below.

- *Housing Relocation* refers to participant responses regarding housing availability, the rebuilding of homes, temporary housing, cost and ability to relocate, and the ability to return home. Responses in this category also address moving and lack of stability, validating the responses to the number of times evacuees have relocated since the storm.
- *Employment* encompasses all responses regarding job availability in both New Orleans and the host city.
- *Infrastructure/Services* comprises a broad range of responses, including the availability of schools, hospitals and health-care facilities, and public utilities. The rebuilding of levees and flood protection are also included in this category of responses, as well as debris removal and road conditions in the city of New Orleans.
- *Transportation* is considered separate from infrastructure/services because of the high incidence of responses in this category regarding the loss of personal transportation. Also included in this category are participant responses regarding the availability of public transportation in the host cities.
- *Leadership/Rebuilding* includes responses regarding communications and messages from local leadership, as well as plans for rebuilding the city by local, state, and federal governments.
- *Emotional/Social* encompasses responses relative to the separation from friends and family, post-disaster stress, the inability to locate family members, uncertainty about the future, and the treatment of evacuees in host cities.
- *Financial Stability* refers to responses relative to insurance, the cost of relocating and rebuilding, the replacement of damaged possessions, and financial recovery.

The question was worded to capture perceptions of evacuees in general, as opposed to the challenges facing the individual respondent (which is addressed later in the survey) with results as illustrated below.

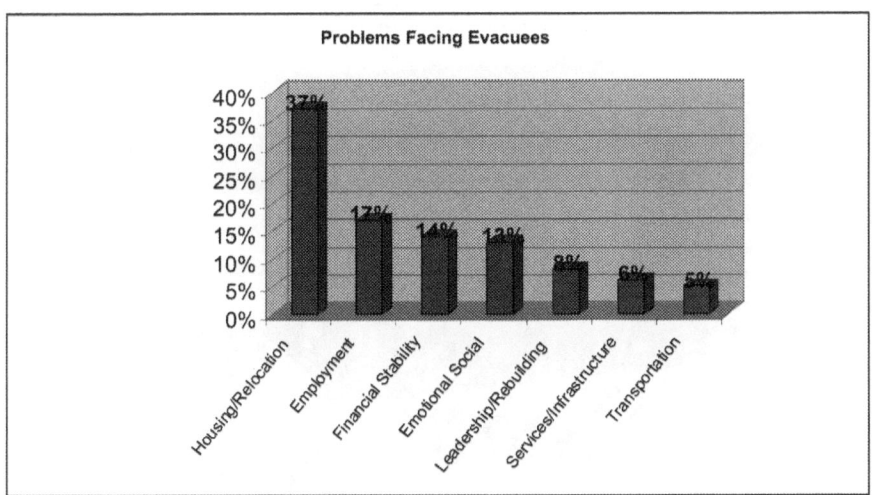

As anticipated, responses regarding housing/relocation appeared most frequently among all participants, followed by employment and financial stability, which were also anticipated as being among the most formidable challenges facing evacuees. Compellingly, emotional/social issues emerged as the fourth most frequent response, unexpectedly higher than responses related to the availability of infrastructure/services and transportation. Also, responses relative to leadership/rebuilding were higher than infrastructure/services, with many of these responses involving communications and conflicting messages from governments.

In the main, the findings were fairly consistent across all categories of respondents, including those that have decided to return to New Orleans and those that have decided not to return, as illustrated below.

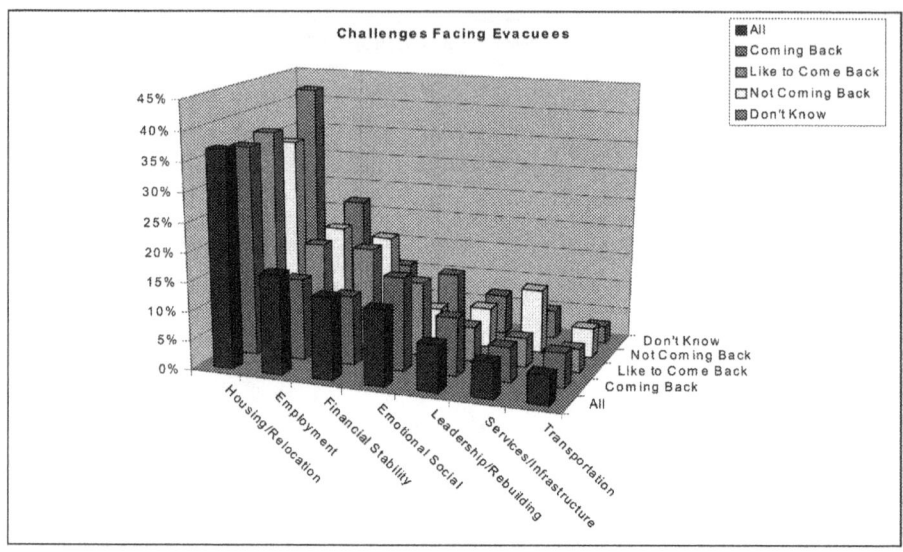

Discernable differences in the frequency of responses are noted among respondents who have decided to return to New Orleans, with a higher frequency of responses regarding financial stability than the responses regarding employment at 16 percent and 12 percent, respectively. This disparity, however, may be attributable to the number of evacuees who are living outside of the city but close enough to commute to work daily. Additionally, these respondents have a higher-than-average response rate regarding emotional/social issues, which may be attributable to their ability to return, while family members and friends are unable to do so; this response rate may also be attributable to conflicts between school-age children and the school-age students of the host cities.

Among respondents who have decided not to return to New Orleans, the frequency of response regarding infrastructure/services was slightly higher, as well as the frequency regarding leadership/rebuilding. Notably, respondents in the not coming back group evidenced a significantly higher incidence of homeownership at 62 percent, as opposed to those that are coming back, would like to come back, and don't know at 48 percent, 37 percent, and 33 percent, respectively. As infrastructure/services includes levees and flood protection, the frequency of this response may be attributable to the high number of uninsured homeowners in the lower-income neighborhoods.

In identifying the factors influencing the decision of individual evacuees to return to New Orleans, an open-ended question was used. It asked respondents to list the three most important factors of their decision, with a follow-up, closed-ended question asking participants to rank a series of thirteen factors on a scale of one to five, with five being the most important.

Analysis of the responses to the open-ended question yielded thirteen distinct themes, as detailed below.

- *New Orleans is Home/Rebuild New Orleans* is characterized by responses such as want to come home, lived there all my life, want to help rebuild, no place like home, own home, family home, etc. Other, more subtle and yet meaningful responses included such statements as I care, have faith, there is no choice, we can overcome, etc.
- *Housing Availability* includes responses relative to the need for housing, the loss of a home, and the devastation of the neighborhood.
- *Flood Protection* encompasses responses regarding levee protection, evacuation plans, the need to know that the levee failure will not happen again, and, to a lesser extent, comments regarding such issues as closing the Mississippi River Gulf Outlet (MRGO) and coastal wetland restoration.
- *Job/Business/Career in New Orleans* is characterized by responses that specify either an existing job or a job waiting in New Orleans. These respondents referred specifically to my job, spouse's job or business, or returning to a specific employer, and long-term employment in a job or industry.
- *Job Availability*, conversely, refers to the ability to get a good job in New Orleans, the necessity to leave a job in a host city, better employment opportunities and higher wages in host cities, or a transfer by an employer.
- *Familial/Social/Cultural Networks* encompasses responses relative to being with friends and family, returning to specific neighborhoods, residing in faith-based communities, and having community pride. References to New Orleans' unique culture were also included in this response category.
- *Finish School/University* is characterized by responses of students from local universities or, in some cases, spouses of university students.

- *School Open/Quality Education* includes the availability of K–12 education for school-age children, as well as the quality of education in host cities.
- *Plan for the Future/Leadership/Politics* includes responses by participants waiting for a rebuilding plan and also includes questions about citizens' uncertainty regarding the rebuilding of specific neighborhoods. Also, comments about local, state, and federal governments and officials, as well as references to political interference in the planning and rebuilding process, are included in this response category.
- *Environmental Quality/Infrastructure/Services* encompasses a variety of responses, including debris removal, air and water quality, restoration of utilities, the availability of health-care services, and the availability of police, fire, and emergency medical services.
- *Affordability/Market/Cost of Living* includes such factors as insurance, cost of housing, financial ability to rebuild without incurring debt, and post-Katrina real estate market values and the ability to sell a home in New Orleans.

Unlike responses to the survey questions regarding challenges to evacuees, the more personal questions regarding factors that influence individual decisions about returning revealed significantly different results across respondent categories. The table below illustrates.

FACTORS INFLUENCING DESCISION TO RETURN	ALL	COMING BACK	LIKE TO COME BACK	NOT COMING BACK	NOT LIKELY TO COME BACK
New Orleans is Home	33%	48%	28%	6%	7%
Familial/Social/Cultural	23%	29%	23%	11%	9%
Housing Availability	11%	3%	15%	22%	24%
Job Availability	11%	6%	11%	20%	18%
Environment/Infrastructure/Services	6%	2%	7%	4%	16%
Job/Business/Career in N.O.	6%	8%	4%	3%	4%
School Open/Quality Education	3%	1%	5%	8%	6%
Flood Protection	3%	1%	2%	14%	7%
Plan for the Future/Leadership	3%	1%	1%	10%	6%
Affordability/Market/Cost	<1%	0%	2%	0%	3%
Finish School/University	<1%	1%	1%	2%	0%

As anticipated, New Orleans is home is the factor most influential in the decision to return by respondents who have decided to return and those who would like to come back at 48 percent and 28 percent, respectively. Family and friends was the second most frequent response at 29 percent and 23 percent, respectively. For respondents who were coming back to New Orleans, job/business/career in New Orleans was the third most frequent response; however, for the like to come home respondent category, housing availability remained a factor impacting the final decision to return to New Orleans.

For those deciding not to return and for the undecided, housing availability (22 percent and 24 percent, respectively) and job availability (20 percent and 18 percent, respectively) were the two factors that most affected the decision. For participants who decided not to return, flood protection was the third most important factor affecting their decision. For participants who were still undecided, environment/infrastructure/service was the third most important factor.

The availability of schools to serve K–12 school-age students was a very low factor influencing the decision to return at 3 percent overall—1 percent for respondents who made the decision to return and 2 percent for those in the like to come home respondent category. However, the findings indicated that 39 percent of survey participants had school-age children in the home. Of the respondents who were coming home and would like to come home, 39 percent and 35 percent, respectively, had school-age children in the home. For those deciding not to return, 47 percent had school-age children, and, for the undecided, 42 percent had school-age children.

Analysis of the closed-ended question, which prioritized specific factors impacting the decision to return, revealed that housing, flood protection, health care, employment, and family were the primary factors affecting the decision to return. Having a place to live was the first priority among all respondent categories. Flood protection ranked second among respondents who were definitely coming back and third among respondents who were not coming back, as well as those who were undecided. For respondents who were not coming back, having a good job and benefits ranked third. For respondents who would like to come back and the undecided, health care ranked as the second most important priority. Finally, being with family and friends ranked third among respondents who were coming back.

	ALL	COMING BACK	LIKE TO COME BACK	NOT COMING BACK	NOT LIKELY TO COME BACK
Housing	1	1	1	1	1
Environment	4	7	6	2	4
Employment	9	10	9	3	10
Leadership	12	12	12	12	11
Schools	11	8	7	7	12
Family	6	3	5	10	6
Flood Protection	2	2	3	6	3
Childcare	14	14	14	13	14
Police Protection	7	9	8	4	9
Health Care	3	5	2	5	2
Street Lighting	10	11	11	9	7
Culture	13	13	13	14	13
Businesses Open	5	6	4	8	8
City Services	8	4	10	11	5

Here again, the availability of K–12 education and child care indicated a much lower than expected priority among survey participants in all response categories. However, factoring only single heads of households among employed and unemployed females, the analysis yielded having schools open and quality childcare as higher priorities, as illustrated below.

	Employed Female Head of Household	Unemployed Female Head of Household
Housing	1	1
Environment	6	5
Employment	2	8
Leadership	12	14
Schools	4	3
Family	7	5
Flood Protection	8	6
Childcare	10	4
Police Protection	5	11
Health Care	3	2
Street Lighting	12	10
Culture	14	12
Businesses Open	9	9
City Services	11	13

For employed female heads of households, pre-Katrina housing, employment, and health care were the three top priorities, with schools open ranking fourth. These findings may be attributable to the extensive K–12 parochial education system in New Orleans that is limited by the dependence of working families on the public school system. For unemployed female heads of households, housing, health care, and schools were the three top priorities, with child care as the fourth priority. These findings may indicate the need for childcare options for parents seeking employment or possibly the need for more infant and toddler childcare.

Finally, with regard to the factors influencing the decision to return, the data indicated a high frequency of health care in the prioritization of decision factors.

Recommendations for Rebuilding New Orleans

In the areas of housing, childcare, employment, public safety, leadership, education, and neighborhoods, survey participants were asked to provide suggestions on what should be done in New Orleans. The open-ended question resulted in three to five basic recommendations in each area.

In the area of housing, four distinct themes emerged. More housing was the most prevalent at 91 percent of respondent recommendations and included such responses as affordable housing for the poor, increased home ownership, reopening public housing, etc. Stronger structures also emerged as a key theme at 1 percent, with survey respondents recommending housing built to withstand storm winds. Temporary housing included such recommendations as FEMA trailers and the utilization of public and private property for the placement of trailers. Housing services at 8 percent emerged as a key theme, encompassing such issues as permits, information on building codes, and insurance.

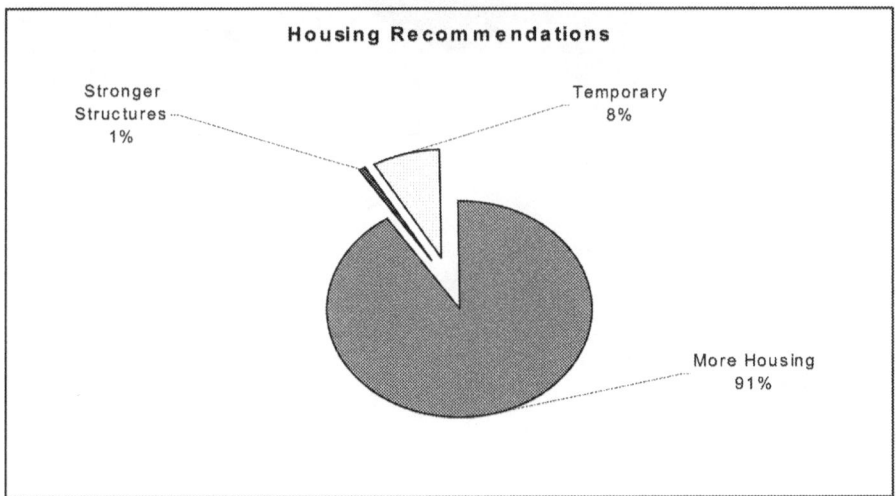

Two themes emerged in the recommendations regarding childcare: more affordable childcare at 84 percent, including extended hours and Head Start, and qualified childcare providers and certified programs (coded as Caregiver) at 16 percent.

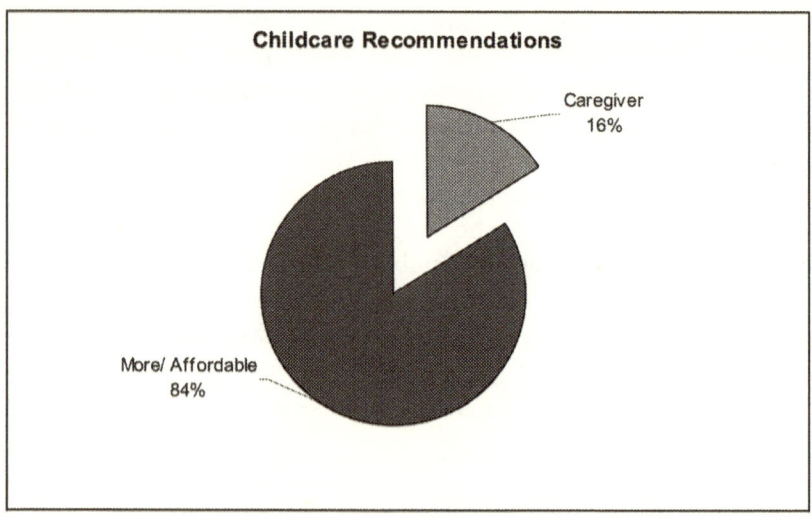

For employment, the themes that emerged included wages, training and placement, availability of jobs, and benefits. Recommendations focusing on wages included higher, competitive, and living wages, as well as increased minimum wage. Training and placement included both occupational skill training and the availability of job placement centers. Availability of jobs included the broadest range of responses, such as equal opportunity, diversity in businesses, the attracting of new businesses, and hiring preferences for local citizens in the rebuilding process. Lastly, benefits included such recommendations as health care, benefit packages, and better working environments.

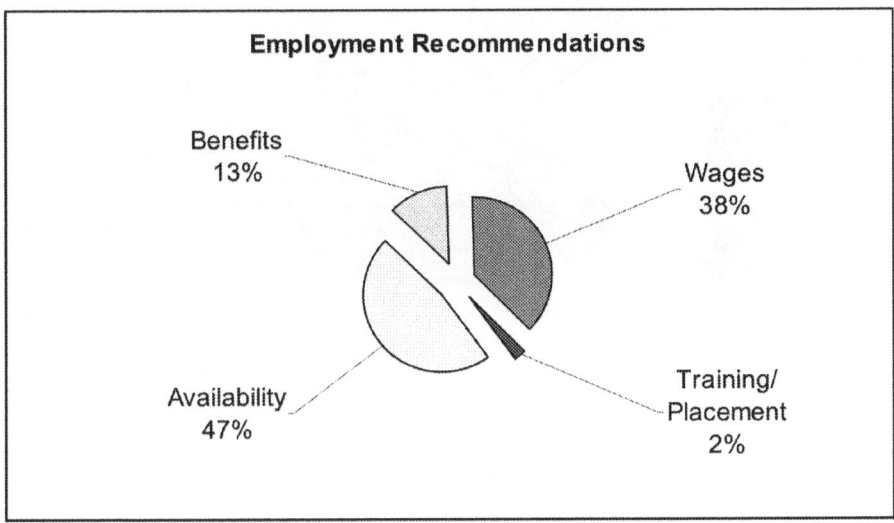

Around the issue of public safety, emerging themes included more police and fire protection services (60 percent), better training for police (16 percent), better leadership in the police department (9 percent), and environmental and infrastructure protection, such as levee protection, street lighting, and emergency preparedness (15 percent).

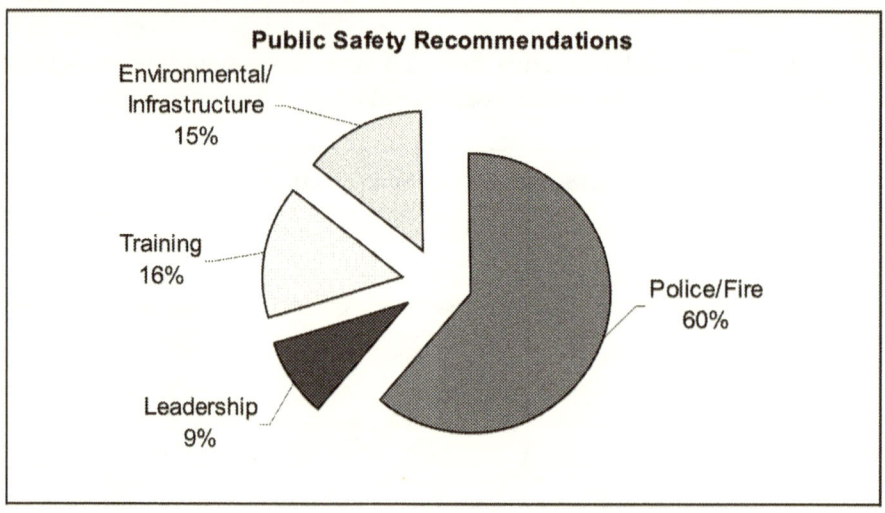

Leadership produced three areas of recommendations. At 72 percent, turnover included recommendations for new, better, or stronger leaders. Communications included recommendations by respondents for better inter-governmental communications, more community involvement in decision making, and improved government responsiveness to citizens at 27 percent. Lawmaking as a leadership theme at only 1 percent included recommendations around better policy and more effective lawmaking by elected officials.

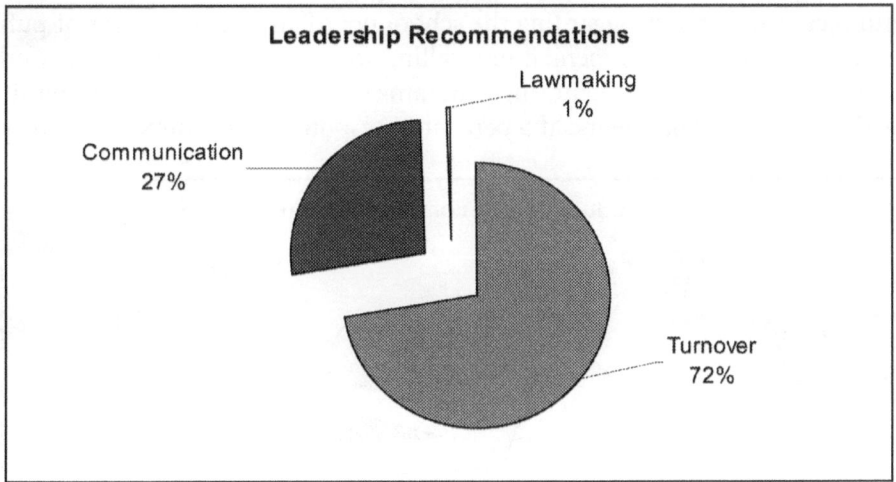

In the area of education or schools, the most prevalent theme emerging in the recommendations at 69 percent called for new, more, or better schools. Recommendations such as decreasing overcrowding, being competitive with other school systems, having quality education in all neighborhoods, etc., were included in this theme. Additionally, increasing teacher qualifications and pay emerged in the recommendations at 21 percent.

Similar to public safety, leadership emerged as a key theme at 5 percent with recommendations regarding the school board and state takeover of public schools. Lastly, recommendations calling for parental involvement, youth programs, tutoring, and mentoring programs were included in the community participation response theme at 5 percent of respondent recommendations.

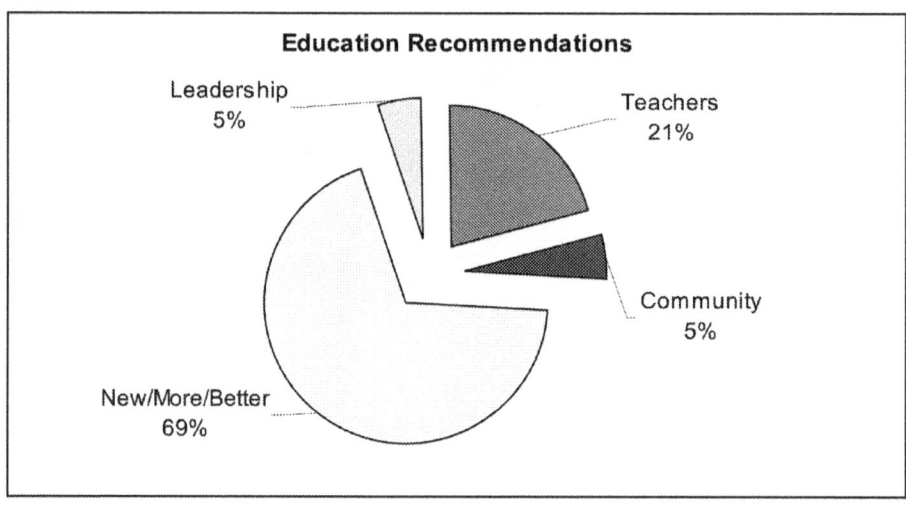

Education Recommendations

Leadership 5%

Teachers 21%

Community 5%

New/More/Better 69%

Finally, three themes emerged in the recommendations for New Orleans neighborhoods. Safer/cleaner neighborhoods emerged as the prevalent theme at 58 percent, including such recommendations as clean streets, less blight, increased accountability of property owners, and an improvement in potholes, street lighting, and police presence. Recommendations calling for neighborhood watch programs, neighborhood clinics, booster clubs and little league in parks and playgrounds, and community participation emerged as a key theme at 41 percent (coded as Community). Density/diversity as a theme included recommendations for the maintenance of the demographic makeup of neighborhoods, smaller and less dense communities, and the preservation of neighborhood culture at 1 percent.

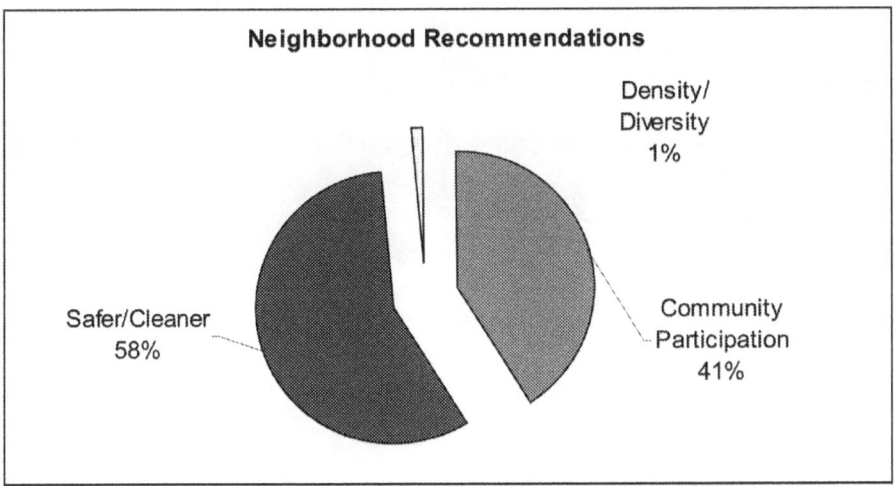

Involvement of and Communications with Citizens

The survey questioned participants regarding their perceptions of citizens' involvement in the planning for rebuilding New Orleans. Additionally, the effectiveness of communication with citizens, as well as citizens' perception of the reliability of communications mechanisms, was addressed.

In the main, the majority of survey participants perceived little or no involvement of citizens in the planning process for rebuilding New Orleans, as illustrated below.

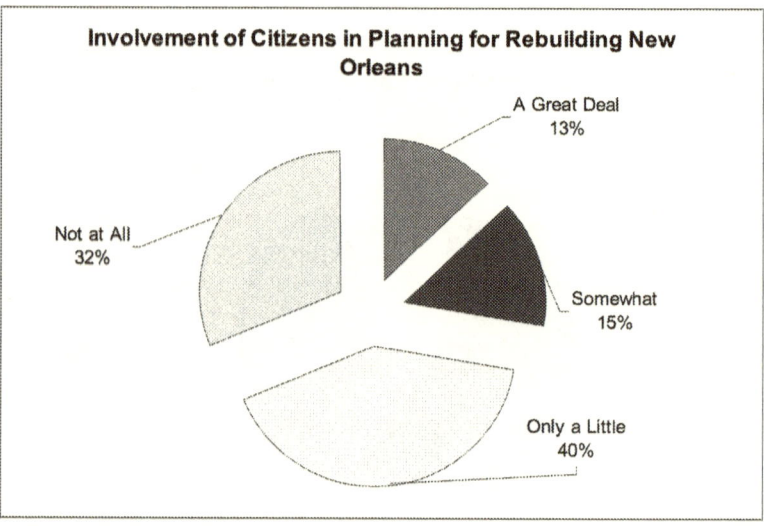

Additionally, in ascertaining information about the best method for educating and informing citizens, survey participants were asked to rank a number of communications media, including print and electronic media, faith-and community-based organizations, friends and relatives, and town hall meetings. However, among the seven methods listed, there was no real discernable difference between the responses, which ranged from 11 percent to 14 percent. Notably, print and electronic media and faith-based institutions were identified as the most effective method at 14 percent.

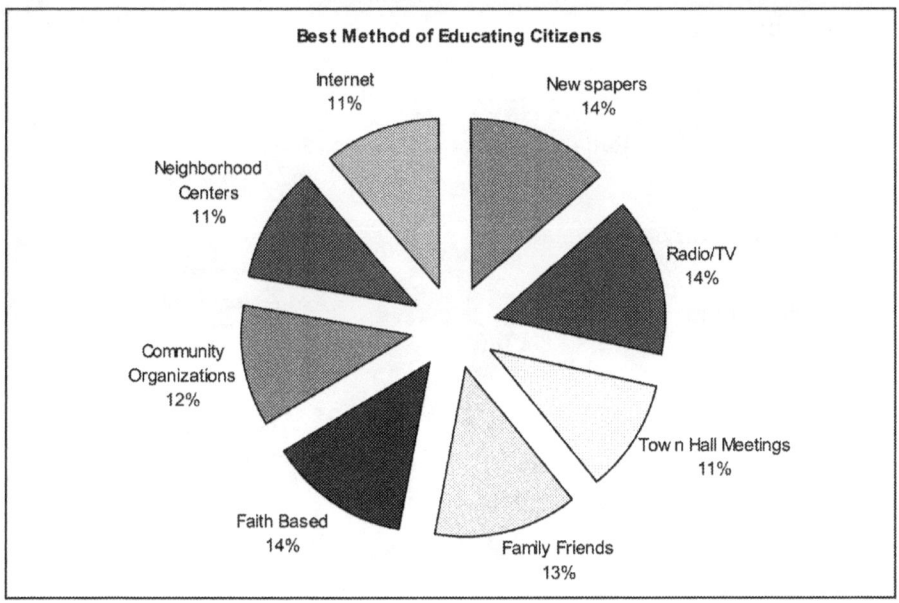

Similar results were evidenced in participant responses to questions regarding the most reliable sources of information. Survey participants were asked to provide information on the reliability of print and electronic media; local, state, and federal officials; faith-and community-based institutions; and family and friends in providing trustworthy information. Here again there was no discernable difference with responses ranging from 6 percent for local, state, and federal officials (including FEMA) to 10 percent for print and electronic media and family and friends. It is noteworthy, however, that in questions regarding the best methods for educating citizens and the most reliable sources of information, print and electronic media ranked highest, followed by faith-based institutions and friends and family.

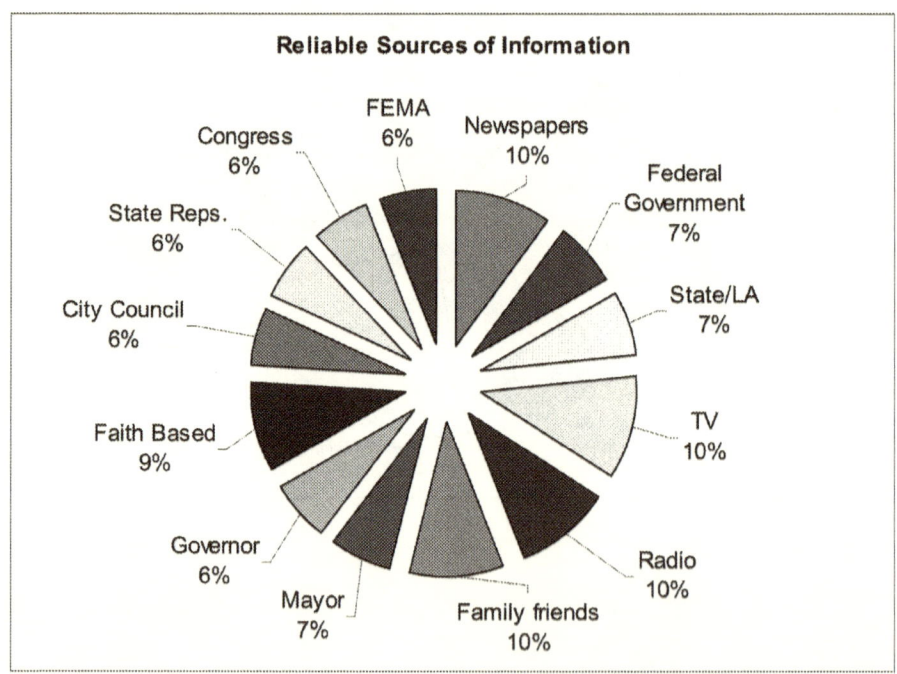

Reliable Sources of Information

FEMA 6%
Congress 6%
Newspapers 10%
State Reps. 6%
Federal Government 7%
City Council 6%
State/LA 7%
Faith Based 9%
TV 10%
Governor 6%
Radio 10%
Mayor 7%
Family friends 10%

Confidence in Government and Rebuilding Poor Communities

In determining citizens' perceptions regarding the interest and ability of the government and community-based organizations to serve poor citizens and poor communities, survey participants were asked to answer a series of questions regarding the understanding of the needs of the poor, commitment to rebuilding poor communities, communications, trust and respect between government and community-based organizations, and the effective handling of issues of race.

In the main, survey participants had negative perceptions of the support for poor communities and efforts to help reduce poverty, with 74 percent of the responses being negative and only 26 percent of the respondents indicating confidence in the willingness and ability of government, CBOs, and the business community to reduce poverty and deal effectively with the issue of race. Of the seventeen issues examined in the area of citizens' confidence in government and the rebuilding of poor communities, only one area elicited a positive response—citizens' support of rebuilding poor communities—with 60 percent of the survey respondents indicating a belief that the citizens of New Orleans are willing to rebuild. All other areas elicited negative responses by 63 percent–88 percent of the survey participants.

Regarding the local government's understanding of the needs of the community and the city at large, participants expressed little confidence. Notably, there was little difference in citizens' perceptions relative to specific community needs and citywide needs, suggesting an overall lack of confidence in the government. Also, in terms of support for the rebuilding of poor communities, here again, respondents expressed little confidence in the government. Conversely, a majority of the respondents expressed confidence in the commitment of the citizens.

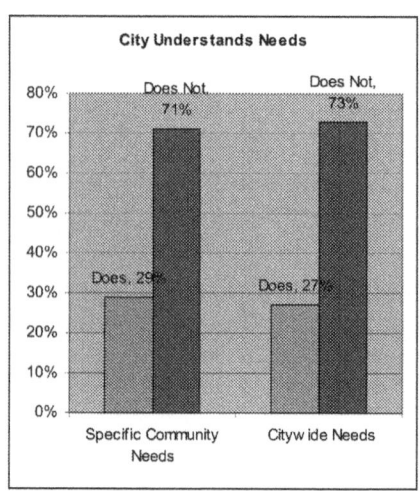

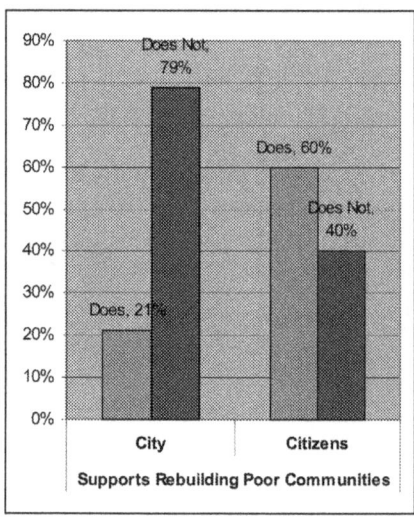

Responses to questions involving race and poverty revealed the same lack of confidence in local leadership, including government, business, and community leadership. While confidence in community leaders' and residents' ability to deal with the issue of race was considerably higher than that of the city government and the business community, the majority of respondents expressed a negative view regarding the ability to deal with the issue of race at any level.

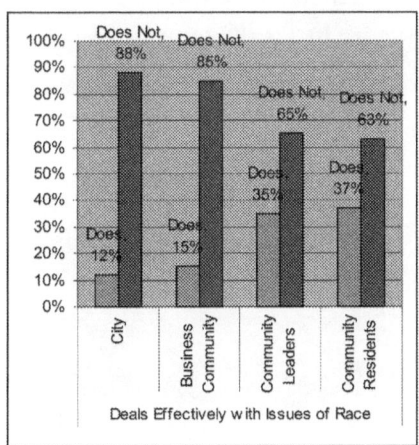

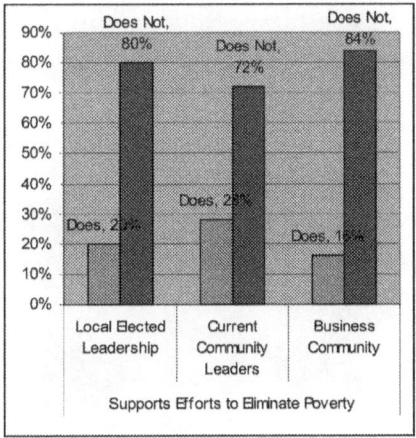

In ascertaining citizens' perceptions of the relationship between government and community-based organizations, the issues of communication, trust, respect, and the efforts to reduce poverty were queried in the survey with unexpected results, given the number of CBOs providing service to New Orleans' poor citizens prior to the storm. The results indicated that with the great number providing services to poor citizens, the respondents didn't feel that CBOs were sincere in their efforts. Additionally, statements regarding the capacity of the city to achieve results and provide resources to alleviate poverty, the majority of the participants responded negatively, particularly regarding the funding of poverty reduction efforts.

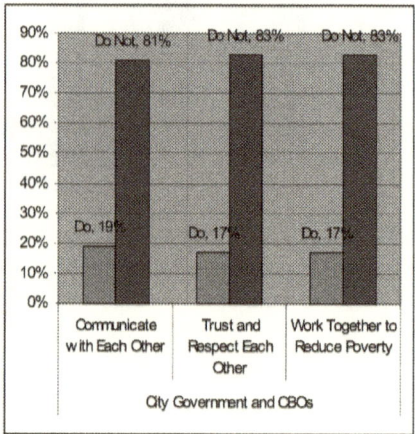 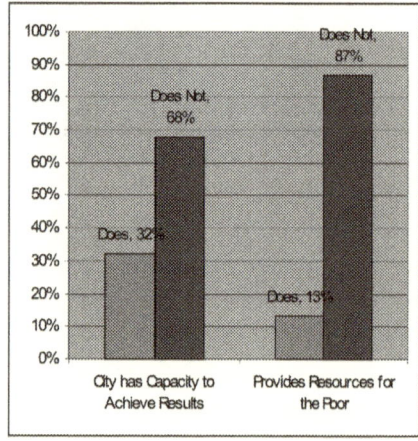

Willingness to Reinvest

To ascertain the areas of community building in which citizens would invest, a list of eleven investment areas were presented and citizens were asked if they would support increased taxes to pay for the infrastructure/services. Initial analysis of data indicated overwhelming support for increased taxes to support better services.

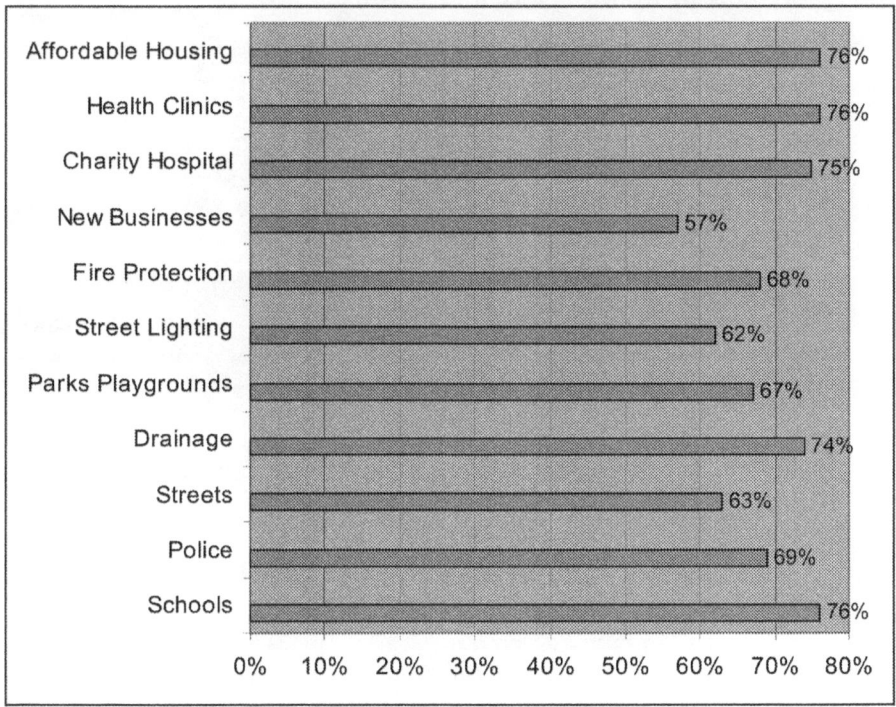

However, controlling for employment status, the analysis revealed that unemployed participants were more likely to support higher taxes for better services, particularly for investment in neighborhood health clinics (54 percent), better schools (53 percent), affordable housing (53 percent), and the rebuilding of Charity Hospital (52 percent). Overall, support for higher taxes among unemployed participants ranged from 39 percent to 54 percent. Conversely, support for higher taxes among employed participants revealed significantly less support, ranging from 18 percent to 24 percent.

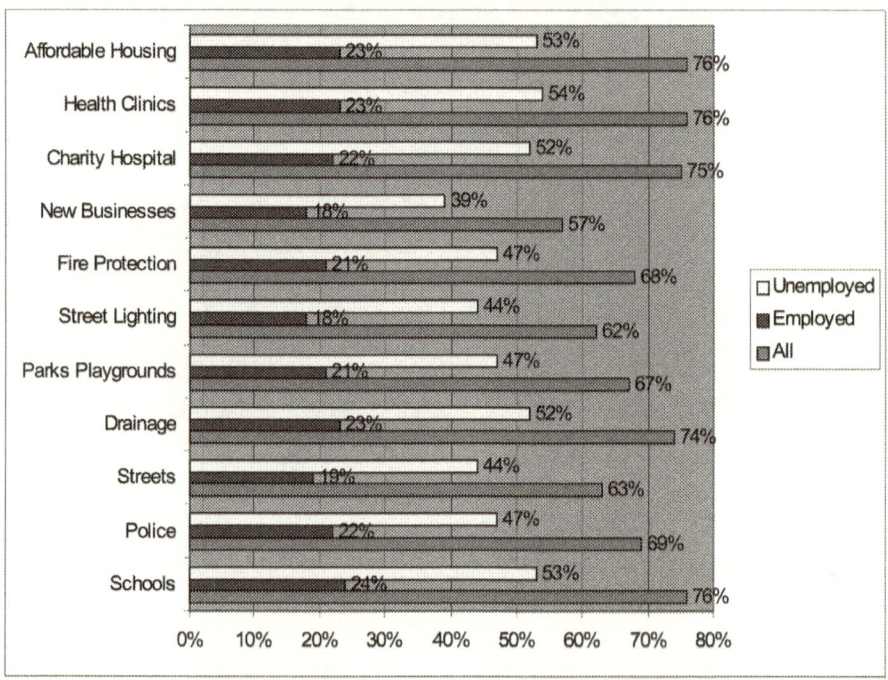

ACTIONABLE RECOMMENDATIONS

With regard to actionable findings, five key issues are indicated in the analysis of the survey data: (1) need for housing; (2) decision of unemployed residents to return; (3) prioritization of childcare in the factors influencing the decision of unemployed female heads of households; (4) prioritization of health care as a factor influencing the decision to return; and (5) lack of confidence in government, business community, community based organizations, and community leaders in rebuilding poor communities.

First and foremost, the availability of housing is the number one factor influencing the decision of low-to moderate-income citizens to return to New Orleans and the most actionable finding of the survey. Given the slow pace of providing temporary housing via FEMA trailers and the not-in-my-backyard (NIMBY) response from many New Orleans neighborhoods, reopening New Orleans Public Housing Development is an immediate and necessary step for bringing evacuees back to New Orleans. Additionally, prior to Hurricane Katrina, New Orleans had over twenty thousand blighted and/or abandoned properties, many in higher elevation areas of the city. Making these sites immediately available for either transitional housing or redevelopment must be a priority in bringing New Orleans' citizens, particularly low-to moderate-income and working poor, back home.

The housing issue is further exacerbated by pre-Katrina data, which indicates that thirty-three out of every one hundred people who lived in New Orleans were poor. This demographic reality of pre-Katrina New Orleans, coupled with the fact that a significant percentage of low-income and unemployed citizens indicates that they are definitely returning to New Orleans, further informs the development of actionable steps to take in order to assist low-income people. Tellingly, if this finding pans out, it would mean the reassembling of large disparities in assets, i.e., homeownership, savings, investments, operation of businesses, education levels, etc., which has existed in New Orleans, almost at the same level, for more than fifty-five years.

To help reverse the historic disparities that plagued pre-Katrina New Orleans and threatened the city's post-Katrina recovery, two of the eight recommendations on poverty reduction provided by TCA are actionable and meaningful based on the findings of the survey.

- The city of New Orleans and the state of Louisiana, using acceptable citizen participation models and best practices of policy development, must adopt an official policy on poverty reduction as a part of their economic development strategy.

- The city of New Orleans should use a percentage of its Community Development Block Grant (CDBG) funds to induce private/public partnerships to tailor their fringe benefits to help income-eligible workers to build assets. Four examples of asset-building projects offered are
  - ➤ TCA, Inc., and Liberty Bank's Individual Development Account project (IDA);
  - ➤ TCA, Inc., and First Bank and Trust's IDA project;
  - ➤ Harrah's project for first-time homeownership and education (It is strongly recommended that the New Orleans City Council closely enforce and monitor the requirements of the project and its results, as well as urge that the project be tweaked when required.) The program was designed by Dr. Peter W. Dangerfield, Jr., using TCA's Poverty-Reduction Model; and
  - ➤ Pampy's Crystal Catering's IDA assistance for workers

The IDA initiative should be citywide. Moreover, its aim should be asset building through the ownership of businesses and homes and through education. Further, it is recommended that, identical to Mt. Auburn Associates findings, an IDA initiative is instituted that assists large numbers of families, (i.e., 1,000/5,000/10,000) that will either 3,000,000 / 15,000,000 / 30,000,000 plus program administration costs depending on the number of families helped. The program will have a three-to-one match. Most importantly, it is strongly recommended that the influx of new and other unprogrammed CDBG funds be used to pay for the initiative. (Sources used must be recurring funds, and asset building must be an eligible cost. Otherwise, the maintenance of a fund stream becomes the focus and asset building becomes supplanted.)

A second major actionable item concerns the finding that among low-and moderate-income evacuees, unemployed residents are more likely to have made the decision to return than employed residents. Compellingly, these findings suggest that effective programs for job training and job placement will be required to assist returning low-and moderate-income evacuees. A similar finding was offered by Mt. Auburn, a firm that has spent the past year studying the economic recovery effort in New York following 9/11. They state

> Quick turnaround training needs to be developed to support skill development in occupations that are currently in greatest demand. This training needs to be made available to those who have returned, as well as to displaced residents wishing to return and take advantage of new opportunities for increasing their employment opportunities.[3]

TCA continues to recommends
- Implement a case management system to identify critical needs of displaced people, and target resources to meet those needs; also, promote intense formal linkage and coordination among cooperating entities
- Provide support to ensure the resources needed to play a critical role in meeting the immediate training needs of residents
- Provide training sites to encourage displaced residents interested in new skill development to return for training
- Develop specialized training in construction, historic preservation, and other trades related to rebuilding

Additionally, among unemployed female heads of households, childcare ranked as a high priority in the factors influencing the decision to return. As such, this finding supports the recommendation that childcare options be made available for unemployed job seekers while both searching and training for jobs. Also, this finding suggests that a more detailed examination of childcare needs to be conducted to determine the need for infant and toddler care, or nontraditional childcare options must be made available, such as evening care for young children.

An additional factor that must be considered in the finding regarding the decision of unemployed evacuees to return to New Orleans is the potential for increased crime. Given that returning evacuees are already dealing with a myriad of emotional, social, and economic issues caused by relocation, hotel evictions, the limitations of FEMA temporary housing assistance, a lack of

---

3   Bringing New Orleans Back Economic Development Plan, input from Mt. Auburn Associates, January 2006.

affordable housing options, a lack of available education options for senior high school students, and unemployment, local communities must be prepared for the prevention and intervention of drug-related and domestic violence-related crime.

Finally, with regard to the decision by employed low-to moderate-income workers to return, the data suggests that New Orleans' working poor are less likely to return than the non-working poor. It can be assumed from the finding that wages for low-and moderately-skilled workers in host cities are higher and more attractive than wages in New Orleans' service-based economy. Notably, among the first recovery policies enacted by the federal government for rebuilding New Orleans was the suspension of the Davis Bacon Wage Act, leaving both skilled and unskilled workers without wage protection for federally funded recovery and rebuilding efforts. While the labor market supply shortage has inflated wages across industry sectors, policies and programs that ensure more competitive wages and compensation for workers, including benefit packages, are needed to facilitate the repopulation of the city by New Orleans' residents.

Health care ranked high in the prioritization of factors influencing the decision to return, supporting the notion that the Charity Hospital system serves as the primary health-care provider for uninsured families. Notably, long-term plans proposed by both local and state recovery authorities call for the development of neighborhood clinics as a viable alternative to Charity Hospital and clinics. However, until such time as neighborhood health clinics are available, many uninsured New Orleanians perceive an absence of health-care options for themselves and their families.

Last, but certainly not least, the data overwhelmingly indicates that low-to moderate-income citizens have a lack of confidence in elected government, business, and community leadership. With regard to sources of reliable information, low-and moderate-income citizens express higher confidence in print and electronic media than in elected or community leaders. Also, questions regarding perceptions of elected, business, and community leaders' commitment to rebuilding poor communities reveal that most evacuees have little hope that their interests are a priority for anyone but themselves. Clearly, the data indicates a need for extensive outreach and communications targeting low-and moderate-income evacuees. Moreover, the findings suggest that outreach to and communications with New Orleans evacuees must extend beyond government and elected officials and must include business, as well as faith- and community-based leadership.

APPENDIX A

I. Heading for Questionnaire

Citizen Participation to Inform Policy on Rebuilding New Orleans

Name	Current City, State, Zip
New Orleans Street Address	New Orleans Zip Code

II.   Plans for Returning to New Orleans—Sample Questions

(Record Exact Words)

1.   What do you think is the most important problem facing dislocated people?

_____

_____ ☐☐

2.   What do you think is the second most important problem facing dislocated people today?

_____

_____ ☐☐

3.   Please check the box that best describes your plans about coming back to New Orleans.

I am definitely coming back. ☐   I would like to come back. ☐   I am not coming back. ☐   Undecided ☐

4.   Please tell us the 3 most important reasons for your decision. (If you are undecided, what reasons will most influence your decision?)

_____

_____

_____

5.   In general, to what extent do you feel citizens of New Orleans are included in planning efforts aimed at cleaning up and rebuilding?

a.	A Great Deal	1	_____
b.	Somewhat	2	_____
c.	Only a Little	3	_____
d.	Not at All	4	_____
e.	Don't Know	5	_____

III.   Impediments to Returning to New Orleans— Sample Questions

Overall, on a scale of 1 to 5, with 1 being least important and 5 being most important, please tell us how important each of the following factors is to your decision to come back to New Orleans.

	Least Important 1	2	3	4	Most Important 5	Don't Know
Housing						
Environment & Cleanup						
Jobs & Economy						

Leadership & Vision						
Education						
Being with Family & Friends						
Flood Protection						
Quality Child Care						
New Orleans' Culture						
Salary & Fringe Benefits						
Police Protection						
Street Lighting						
Adequate Hospitals						

IV.   Perceptions on Leadership—Sample Questions

Give 2 to 3 suggestions for each area listed below that you feel are needed to clean up or rebuild New Orleans.

Day Care/Schooling

_____

_____

_____

Housing

_____

_____

_____

Employment

_____

_____

_____

Law Enforcement

_____

_____

_____

Leadership

_____

_____

_____

V. Views on What Needs to be Done to Clean Up and Rebuild New Orleans

1. In your opinion, what is the main issue in the efforts to clean up and rebuild New Orleans?

    _____

    _____

    _____

         ☐☐

2. In your opinion, what is the main issue of poor people in the cleaning up and rebuilding efforts of New Orleans?

    _____

    _____

    _____

         ☐☐

3. What should be the top priority in the cleanup and rebuilding of New Orleans? (Circle the appropriate number, with 1 being most important and 4 the least important.)

a. Strict Enforcement of Laws	1	2	3	4
b. Housing	1	2	3	4
c. Schools	1	2	3	4
d. Employment	1	2	3	4
e. Communication of City's Vision/Plans	1	2	3	4
f. Coordination between City, State, and Federal Government	1	2	3	4
g. Other (specify)	1	2	3	4

4. Think about the statements below in the context of poverty reduction and community revitalization efforts in your city. (Circle the phrase (a or b) that best completes each statement about city government and the overall conditions in your city.

a. City government (a) DOES/(b) DOES NOT understand specific community needs.

b. City government (a) DOES/(b) DOES NOT understand citywide needs.

c. City government (a) IS/(b) IS NOT committed to poverty reduction efforts.

d. City government (a) DOES/(b) DOES NOT deal effectively with issues of race/ethnicity.

e. City government (a) DOES/(b) DOES NOT exhibit an excessive need for control.

f.   City government (a) DOES/(b) DOES NOT have the capacity to achieve results.

g.   City government (a) IS/(b) IS NOT overly bureaucratic.

h.   City government (a) DOES/(b) DOES NOT provide adequate resources/funding.

i.   City government (a) DOES/(b) DOES NOT communicate effectively among themselves.

j.   City government (a) DOES/(b) DOES NOT emphasize different program areas.

k.   City government (a) DOES/(b) DOES NOT work at different project/program scopes.

l.   Community residents (a) DO/(b) DO NOT support poverty reduction efforts.

m.   The local political environment (a) DOES/(b) DOES NOT support poverty reduction efforts.

n.   Current local elected leadership (a) DOES/(b) DOES NOT support poverty reduction efforts.

o.   Current community leadership (a) DOES/(b) DOES NOT support poverty reduction efforts.

p.   Existing community institutions (a) DO/(b) DO NOT support poverty reduction efforts.

q.   Local businesses/private industry (a) DO/(b) DO NOT support poverty reduction efforts.

r.   Community leaders (a) DO/(b) DO NOT deal effectively with race/ethnicity issues.

s.   Community residents (a) DO/(b) DO NOT deal effectively with race/ethnicity issues.

5.   Using the following scale, please indicate how strongly you agree or disagree with the following statements.
Strongly Agree = SA (4), Agree = A (3), Neutral = N (2), Disagree = DA (1), Strongly Disagree = SDA (0)

	SA	A	N	DA	SDA
a. Need more Law Enforcement	4	3	2	1	0
b. Need more Housing	4	3	2	1	0
c. Need more Schools	4	3	2	1	0
d. Need more Employment	4	3	2	1	0
e. Need more	4	3	2	1	0

6.   What priority should each of the following have in New Orleans?

	High Priority	Medium Priority	Low Priority	Don't Know
a.	3	2	1	0

3	2	1	0
3	2	1	0
3	2	1	0

---

7. How important do you think it is to preserve the racial mix in New Orleans?
   - ❏ Extremely Important
   - ❏ Moderately Important
   - ❏ Slightly Important
   - ❏ Not At All Important

8. How important do you think it is for all evacuees to return to New Orleans?
   - ❏ Extremely Important
   - ❏ Moderately Important
   - ❏ Slightly Important
   - ❏ Not At All Important

9. How would you rate the following services in New Orleans?

	Exceptional	Adequate	Inadequate	Don't Know
a. Parks	3	2	1	0
b. Water System	3	2	1	0
c. Street Maintenance	3	2	1	0
d. Garbage Collection	3	2	1	0
e. Fire Protection	3	2	1	0
f. Police Protection	3	2	1	0
g. Ambulance Service	3	2	1	0
h. Building Inspection	3	2	1	0
i. Animal Control	3	2	1	0
j. Other Code Enforcement (weeds, junk cars, etc.)	3	2	1	0
k. Arts	3	2	1	0
l. Street Lighting	3	2	1	0

10. Below is a list of services that generally require taxes for maintenance and construction. Would you be willing to pay more taxes if you knew the money would be spent in New Orleans for that particular purpose? (Circle one. 1=Yes or 2=No)

	Yes	No
a To Provide Additional Parks	1	0
b. To Upgrade Existing Parks	1	0
c. To Improve Water Service	1	0
d. To Improve Streets and Roads	1	0
e. To Improve Fire Protection	1	0

f. To Improve Police Protection	1	0
g. To Improve Ambulance Service	1	0
h. To Improve Street Lighting	1	0
i. To Provide Recreation Facilities	1	0
j. To Expand the Service Area of a Pressurized Secondary Water System	1	0
k. To Expand and Improve the Storm and Ground Water Drainage System	1	0
l. To Build New and Repair Old Sidewalks in Existing Areas	1	0

11. What do you feel represent the top challenges to elected officials in the next two years? (Select up to three. Number your selections from 1=Most Challenging to 3= Least Challenging.)

❑ Recruitment and Selection of
  Qualified Personnel
❑ Education   ❑ Housing
❑ Community Relations   ❑ Adaptation of New Technology
❑ Program Funding   ❑ Jobs
❑ Interagency/   ❑ Health care
  Intergovernmental   ❑ Health care
  Relations   ❑ Privatization
❑ Demand for Services   ❑ Other (specify) _____
❑ General Financing   ❑ Other (specify) _____

---

12. What do you feel represent the top challenges to health care in the next two years? (Select up to three. Number your selections from 1=Most Challenging to 3=Least Challenging.)

❑ Recruitment and Selection of   ❑ Information Management
  Qualified Personnel   ❑ Financing New Technology
❑ Education   ❑ Caring for People with AIDS
❑ Community Relations   ❑ Issues of Death and Dying
❑ Caring for Uninsured/   ❑ IManaged Care Programs
  Underinsured   ❑ Care for the Elderly
❑ Medical Staff Relations   ❑ Other (specify) _____

13. What do you see as the most significant strengths of the city of New Orleans? (In those areas that you may see as strengths, please select no

more than 2 in the category listed below. Number your answers 1=Most Significant or 2=Least Significant.)

❏ Diverse Culture
❏ Shipping Docks   ❏ Employment Opportunities
❏ Number of Universities ❏ Other (specify) _____
❏ Public School System   ❏ Other (specify) _____

VI.   Source of Information on Conditions in New Orleans Caused by Hurricane Katrina—Sample Questions

1.   Of the sources listed below, what are the three sources of information you feel are most reliable? Sample Questions

	Exceptional	Adequate	Inadequate	Don't Know
a. Newspaper	3	2	1	0
b. Communication from Federal Government	3	2	1	0
c. Communication from State Government	3	2	1	0
d. Communication from Radio	3	2	1	0
e. Communication from TV	3	2	1	0

2. Of the sources listed below, what are the 3 sources of information you feel are the least reliable? Sample Questions

	Exceptional	Adequate	Inadequate	Don't Know
a. Newspaper	3	2	1	0
b. Communication from Federal Government	3	2	1	0
c. Communication from State Government	3	2	1	0
d. Communication from Radio	3	2	1	0
e. Communication from TV	3	2	1	0

3. Indicate below which methods you believe are most or least effective at informing citizens about the cleanup and rebuilding efforts in New Orleans.

		Yes	No	Most Beneficial
a.	Newspapers & Magazines	❑	❑	❑
b.	News Accounts on Radio & TV	❑	❑	❑
c.	Town Hall Meetings	❑	❑	❑
d.	Word-of-mouth	❑	❑	❑
e.	Faith-based Institutions	❑	❑	❑
f.	Relatives and/or Friends Living in New Orleans	❑	❑	❑
g.	Public Service Announcements	❑	❑	❑
h.	Community Organizations	❑	❑	❑
i.	Other (specify)	❑	❑	❑

VII.   Interruption in Lifestyle

1. How long have you lived at your current address?

   ❑ Less than 1 Month   ❑ 1–2 Months   ❑ More than 2 Months

2. How many times have you moved during the past 3 months?

3. Before you lived here, where did you live?

   _____   _____   _____
   City/Town   State/Country   Zip

4. What is your address in New Orleans?

   _____   _____   _____   _____
   Address   City   State   Zip

VII.   Demographics

1. Please tell us about you and your family.

Your Age	Under 25	☐	25–34	☐	35–44	☐	45–65	☐	☐
Household Income	Under 15,000	☐	15,000 to 34,000	☐	35,000 to 64,000	☐	65,000 to 89,000	☐ Over 89,000	☐
(Pre-Katrina)									
No. of children under 18	None	☐	1	☐	2	☐	3–4	☐ 5	☐
Your Race	African American	☐	Caucasian/ White	☐	Hispanic	☐	Asian	☐ Other	☐
Marital Status	Married	☐	Single	☐	Divorced	☐	Widowed	☐	☐
Home-ownership	Own	☐	Rent	☐	Other	☐	☐	☐	☐
Your Gender	Male	☐	Female	☐	☐	☐	☐	☐
Single Head of Household	Yes	☐	No	☐	☐	☐	☐	☐

2.   In 2004, did you receive:

		Yes	No
a.	Earned Income Tax Credit	❑	❑
b.	Food Stamps	❑	❑
c.	Child Tax Credit	❑	❑
d.	Aid to Dependent Children	❑	❑
e.	Medicaid	❑	❑
f.	Louisiana Child Health Insurance Program	❑	❑
g.	Kinshipcare	❑	❑
h.	Section 8	❑	❑

3.   Are you currently employed?   ❑   ❑

APPENDIX B

LOCATIONS OF KATRINA/RITA APPLICANTS FROM LOUISIANA, MISSISSIPPI, ALABAMA, AND TEXAS AS OF 12/16/05

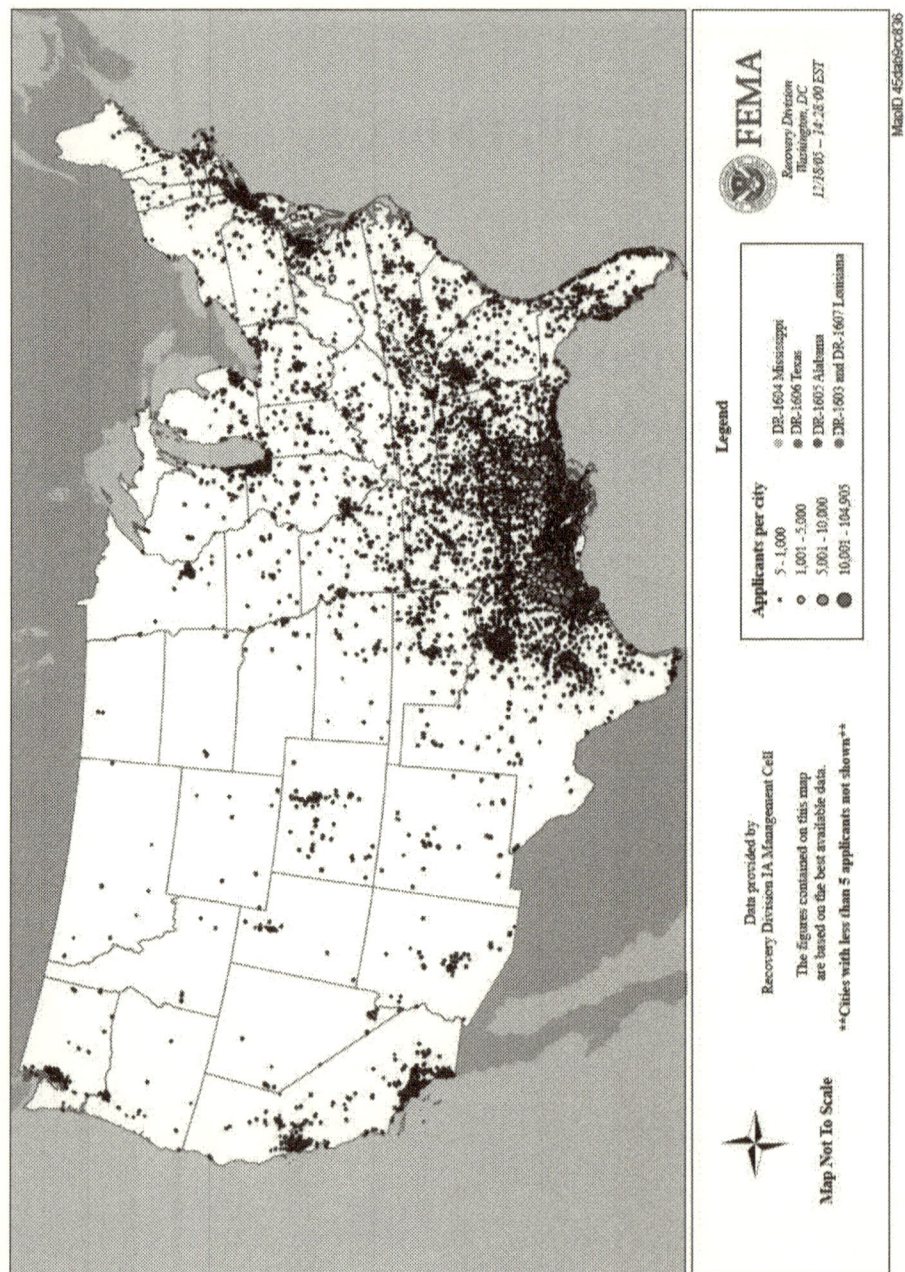

Legend

Applicants per city
· 5 - 1,000
· 1,001 - 5,000
○ 5,001 - 10,000
● 10,001 - 304,905

◈ DR-1604 Mississippi
● DR-1606 Texas
● DR-1605 Alabama
● DR-1603 and DR-1607 Louisiana

Data provided by:
Recovery Division IA Management Cell

The figures contained on this map
are based on the best available data.

Cities with less than 5 applicants not shown

Map Not To Scale

BIBLIOGRAPHY

Alinsky, S. *Rules for Radicals: A Pragmatic Primer for Realistic Radicals.* New York: Vintage Books, 1971.

Alter, C. and Haye, J. *Organizations Working Together.* Newbury Park: Sage Publications, 1993.

Arnstein, Sherry R. "A Ladder of Citizen Participation." *Journal of American Institute of Planners* no. 35, (July 1969).

Arnstein, Sherry R. and Metcalf, E. *Effective Citizen Participation in Transportation Planning, Vol. 2: A Catalog of Techniques.* Washington, DC: U.S. Department of Transportation, Federal Highway Administration, 1976.

Arnstein, S., Gray, J., and Jordan, D. *Effective Citizen Participation in Transportation Planning, Vol. 1: Community Involvement Processes.* Washington, DC: U.S. Transportation, Federal Highway Administration, 1976.

Bachrach, Peter. *The Theory of Democratic Elitism.* Boston: Little Brown, 1967.

Barzelay, M. *Breaking Through Bureaucracy: A New Vision for Managing in Government.* Berkeley: University of California Press, 1992.

Bernstein, Jerome. Manpower—T.W.O. and the Blackstone Rangers. In Edgar Cahn and Barry Passett (Eds.), *Citizen Participation: A Case Book in Democracy.* Trenton: The New Jersey Community Action Training Institute, 1970.

Berry, Jeffrey M., Portney, Kent E., and Thomson, Ken. *The Rebirth of Urban Democracy.* Washington, DC: The Brookings Institution, 1993.

Borden, David. Participation on the Block. In E. S. Cahn and B. A. Passett (Eds.), *Citizen Participation: A Casebook on Democracy*. Trenton, NJ: The New Jersey Community Action Training Institute, 1970.

Box, Richard. *Citizen Governance: Leading American Communities into the 21st Century*. Thousand Oaks: Sage Publications, 1998.

Boyd, D. C. and Gronlund, A. *The Ithaca Model: A Practical Experience in Community-based Planning*. A paper presented at the 1995 Annual TRB meeting in Washington, DC. Available from http://www.ch2m.com/TRB PI/Trr95.doc, 1995.

Boyte, H. C. and Kari, N. N. *Building America: The Democratic Promise of Public Work*. Philadelphia: Temple University Press, 1996.

Cahn, E. S. and Cahn, J. C. Maximum Feasible Participation: A General Overview. In E. S. Cahn & B. A. Passett (Eds.). *Citizen Participation: A Case Book in Democracy*. Trenton: The New Jersey Community Action Institute, 1970.

Cahn, E. S. and Passett, B. A. *Citizen Participation: A Case Book in Democracy* (Rev. ed.). Trenton: The New Jersey Community Action Training Institute, 1970.

Caputo, D. A. and Cole, Richard R. L. "The Public Hearing as an Effective Citizen Participation Mechanism: A Case Study of the General Revenue Sharing Program." *The American Political Science Review* 78, no. 2 (1984): 404–16.

Clark, R. F. *Maximum Feasible Success—A History of the Community Action Program*. Washington, DC: National Association of Community Action Agencies, 2000.

Cleveland, H. "The Twilight of Hierarchy: Speculations on the Global Information Society." *Public Administration Review* no. 45, (1985): 185–95.

Cole, R. L. "Participation in Community Service Organizations." *Research Reports*, (September/October 1981):53–60.

Cooper, T. L. "Citizen participation: From political response to administrative initiative." *The Bureaucrat* 8, no. 40 (Winter 1970–80).

Cooper, T. L. *The Responsible Administrator: An Approach to Ethics for the Administrative Role.* Port Washington: Kennikat Publishing, 1982.

Cooper, T. L. and Radin, B. A. Programs in Public Finance and Policy Analysis. In *From Public Action to Public Administration: Where Does It Lead?* Los Angeles: University of Southern California, 1989.

Cooper, T. C. and Musso, Juliet A. "The Potential for Neighborhood Council Involvement in American Metropolitan Governance." *International Journal of Organization Theory and Behavior* 2, nos. 1 & 2 (1999): 199-232.

Crewe, K. "The Quality of Participatory Design: The Effects of Citizen Input on the Design of the Boston Southwest Corridor." *Journal of the American Planning Association* 67, no. 4 (Autumn 2001): 437.

Crosby, Philip B. *Quality Without Tears: The Art of Hassle Free Management.* New York: McGraw-Hill, 1984.

Crosby, N., Kelly, J. M., and Schaefer, P. Citizens Panels: "A New Approach to Citizen Participation." *Public Administration Review* (March/April 1986): 170-7.

Cummings, T. G. and Worley, C. G. *Organization Development and Change.* Los Angeles: West Publishing Company, 1993.
Cupps, D. S. "Emerging Problems of Citizen Participation." *Public Administration Review* no. 37 (September/October 1987): 478–87.

Dachler, H. P. and Wilpert, B. "Conceptual Dimensions and Boundaries in Participation in Organizations: A Critical Evaluation." *Administrative Science Quarterly* no. 23 (1978): 1-39.

Deming, W. Edwards. *Out of the Crisis.* Cambridge: Center for Advanced Engineering Study, Massachusetts Institute of Technology, 1982.

Drucker, Peter. "What Business Can Learn from Non-profits." *Harvard Business Review* (July/August 1989).

Duram, L. A. and Brown, K. G. "Assessing Public Participation in U.S. Watershed Planning Initiatives." *Society & Natural Resources* no. 12 (1999): 455-467.

Easton, David. *A Framework for Political Analysis.* Englewood Cliffs: Prentice-Hall, 1965.

Easton, D. and Garrity, R. B. "An Approach to the Analysis of Political Systems." *World Politics* no. 9 (1957): 383.

Finer, Herman. Administrative Responsibility in Democratic Government. In Francis Rourke (Ed.), *Bureaucratic Power in National Politics* (pp. 326-336). Boston: Little Brown, 1972.

Follett, Mary Parker. *The New State: Group Organization the Solution of Popular Government.* New York: Longman Green Publishing Company, 1918.

Galbraith, J. R. and Lawler, E. E. III, Introduction: Challenges to the Established Order. *Organizing for the Future: The New Logic for Managing Complex Organizations.* San Francisco: Jossey-Bass, 1993.

Glaser, M. A., Denhardt, K. G., and Grubbs, J. W. "Local Government-sponsored Community Development: Exploring Relationships between Perceptions of Empowerment and Community Impact." *American Review of Public Administration* 27, no. 1, (March 1997): 76-94.

Harris, I. M. "Community Involvement in Desegregation: The Milwaukee Experience." *Journal of Voluntary Action Research* 9, nos. 1–4 (1980): 179-188.

Iglitzin, Lynne B. "The Seattle Commons: A Case Study in the Politics and Planning of an Urban Village." *Policy Studies Journal* 23, no. 4 (Winter 1995): 620–36.

Ishikawa, Kaoru. *What is Total Control? The Japanese Way* (David J. Lu, Trans.). Englewood Cliffs: Prentice-Hall, Inc., 1985.

Johnston, D. *Beyond Bureaucracy: A Blue Print and Vision for Government that Works.* Homewood: Irwin, 1993.

Jun, Jong. *Public Administration Design and Problem Solving.* New York: Macmillan Publishing Company, 1986.

Juran, J. M. and Gryna, Frank M. *Quality Planning and Analysis.* New York: McGraw-Hill, Inc., 1970.

Kamensky, J. M. z'Role of the Reinventing Government Movement in Federal Management Reform." *Public Administration Review* no. 56 (May/June 1996).

Kaufmann, Franz-Xavier (Ed.). *The Public Sector: Challenge for Coordinating and Learning.* Berlin: W. deGruyter., 1991.

Kingsley, D. *Representative Bureaucracy: An Interpretation of the British Civil Service.* Yellow Springs: Antioch University Press, 1944.

Kraut, M. E. and Kraut, R. "The Impact of Citizen Participation on Hazardous Waste Policy Implementation: The Case of Clermont County, Ohio." *Policy Studies Journal* 14, no. 1 (September 1985): 52–61.

Levine, C. "Citizenship and Service Delivery: The Promise of Co-production." *Public Administration* no. 44 (1984): 187.

Lean, M. *Bread, Bricks, Belief: Communities in Charge of Their Future.* West Hartford: Kumarian Press, Inc., 1995.

Lindblom, C. E. "The Science of Muddling Through." *Public Administration Review* no. 19 (Spring 1959).

Luton, L. S. "Citizen Participation in Solid Waste Policymaking: A Case Study of the Spokane Experience." *International Journal of Public Administration* 18, no. 4 (1995): 613–37.

Marston, S. A. and Towers, G. "Private Spaces and the Politics of Places: Spatioeconomic Restructuring and Community Organizing in Tucson and El Paso. In Robert Fisher & Joseph Kling (Eds.), Community-based Mobilizations." *Urban Affairs Annual Review* no. 41 (1993): 75–103.

Mikulecky, Thomas F. "Neighborhoods: Smaller, More Responsive Local Governments." *Public Management* no. 72 (August 1990): 9–10.

Moynihan, D. P. *Maximum Feasible Misunderstanding: Community Action in the War on Poverty.* New York: Free Press, 1969.

Murry, O. and Price, S. *The Greek City from Homer to Alexander.* Oxford: Clarendon Press, 1996.

Musso, J. A. *The Politics of Neighborhood Council Implementation in Los Angeles: Challenges to Participation in a Global City.* Working paper presented at the American Society of Public Administration Annual Conference. San Diego: 1999.

National Partnership for Reinventing Government. *Balancing Measures: Best Practices in Performance Management.* Washington, DC: U.S. Government Printing Office, 1999.

Nunn, S. "Planning for Inner-city Retail Development (Indianapolis case study)." *Journal of the American Planning Association* 67, no. 2 (Spring 2001): 159.

Osborne, D. and Gaebler, T. *Reinventing Government: How the Entrepreneurial Spirit Is Transforming the Public Sector.* Reading: Addison-Wesley Publishing Company, 1992.

Pateman, C. *Participation and Democratic Theory.* Cambridge: Harvard University Press, 1970.

Peters, J. T. and Waterman, Jr., R. H. *In Search of Excellence: Lessons from America's Best-run Companies.* New York: Warner Books, 1982.

Peters, T. "Restoring American Competitiveness: Looking for New Models of Organizations." *Academy of Management Executive* no. 2 (1988): 103–9.

Plumlee, J. P., Starling, J. D., and Kramer, K. W. "Citizen Participation in Water Quality Planning: A Case Study of Perceived Failure." *Administration & Society* 16, no. 4 (February 1985): 455–73.

Putnam, R., Fieldstein, L., and Cohen, D. *Better Together: Restoring the American Community.* New York: Simon and Schuster Adult Publishing Group, 2003.

Rauhe, W. and Thomas S. Lyons. "Towards Creating a Model for Empowering Citizens to Sustain Community Planning and Development Efforts: The Case of Menominee, Michigan, DesignNet Journal 1, Michigan State University, 2000

Reitzes, D. and Reitzes, C. "Two Contemporary Chicago Organizations." *Sociological Quarterly* 28, no. 2 (1987): 265–83.

Renn, O., Webler, T., and Kastenholz, H. "Procedural and Substantive Fairness in Landfill Sitting: A Swiss Case Study." *Risk: Health, Safety, and Environment* no. 7 (Spring 1996): 145–68.

Robertson, Peter J. *Bring the Public in: Client Participation in Public Organization Governance.* Paper presented at the Academy of Management Annual Meeting, Public and Non-Profit Division. Vancouver, B. C., 1995.

Rosener, J. B. "Making Bureaucrats Responsive: A Study of the Impact of Citizen Participation and Staff Recommendations on Regulatory Decision Making." *Public Administration Review* (July/August 1982): 339–45.

Scavo, C. "The Use of Participative Mechanisms by Large U.S. Cities." *Journal of Urban Affairs* no. 15 (1993): 93–109.

Scholtes, P. R. *The Team Handbook*, (21st Printing). Madison: Joiner Associates, Inc., 1988.

Schon, Donald A. *The Reflective Practitioner: How Professionals Think in Action.* Boston: Basic Books, HarperCollins, 1983.

Senge, Peter M. *The Fifth Discipline.* New York: Doubleday, 1990.

Stupak, R. J. "Change, Challenge, and the Responsibility of Public Administrators for Total Quality Management in the 1990s: A Symposium, Part 2." *Public Administration Quarterly* (Spring 1993).

Thomas, John C. *Public Participants in Public Decisions—New Skills and Strategies for Public Managers.* San Francisco: Jossey-Bass Publishers, 1995.

Thomson, K., Berry, Jeffrey M., and Portney, Kent E. *Kernels of Democracy.* Medford: Tufts University, 1994.

Verba, Sidney. *Small Groups and Political Behavior.* Princeton: Princeton University Press, 1961.

Walker, J. L. "A Critique of the Elitist Theory of Democracy." *American Political Science Review* no. 60 (1996): 285.

Weeks, Edward C. "The Practice of Deliberative Democracy: Results from Four Large-scale Trials." *Public Administration Review* 60, no. 4 (July/August 2000): 360–72.

Whitaker, G. P. "Co-production: Citizen Participation in Service Delivery." *Public Administration Review* no. 40 (May/June 1980): 240–6.

ABOUT THE AUTHORS

Dr. Peter W. Dangerfield, Jr. is Executive Director of Total Community Action, Inc., and has served in this capacity for 28 years. Among his primary goals as director of TCA, Inc., is using information from TCA's customers and potential customers to shape policies, building a learning organization that effectively responds to needs of low-income persons in New Orleans, and helping to develop a policy on poverty reduction for the City of New Orleans and State of Louisiana.

Dr. Dangerfield received a Doctorate in Public Administration from the University of Southern California with a concentration in Citizen Participation and Customer Input. He earned a Master's Degree in Political Science with an emphasis in Public Administration from Louisiana State University in New Orleans, a Master's Degree in Quality Management from Loyola University in New Orleans, a Master's Degree in Public Administration from the University of Southern California, and a Master's Degree in Liberal Arts from Tulane University.

Dr. Dangerfield's other experiences include authoring the original Open Access Plan used by the City of New Orleans and Harrah's and serving as one of three liaisons for the New Orleans Disparity Study, as well as lead author on Citizen Participation: Informing Public Policy for Rebuilding New Orleans, and Poverty Reduction–A Plan for Louisiana.

Mr. J. Kelley Terry is a founding principal of KL&M Company and has more than fifteen years of diverse planning experience through various projects, managing and providing technical assistance for visioning, comprehensive planning, economic development, and non-profit management. He is a member and officer of various planning and developing committees and has served as an adjunct faculty member and assistant professor at Dillard University. Mr. Terry also holds a bachelor's and master's degree and is in the final stages of study working toward a doctorate in urban development. He has membership in the American Institute of Certified Planners and Immediate Past National Chair of the Planning and the Black Community Division of APA. He holds a

Masters of Urban Planning from the University of Kansas and Bachelor of Arts in Urban Studies from Jackson State University.

Judith Williams has more than twenty years of professional and technical experience in the private and public sectors. As a marketing consultant with a major telecommunications corporation, her skills and expertise were acquired through extensive training and successful engagement with both public and private sector customers. She has completed course work at several universities and has extensive training in marketing, marketing research, and quality management. Ms. Williams' current involvement in this area includes facilitating a $35 million mitigation program funded by the Army Corps of Engineers.

ABOUT TOTAL COMMUNITY ACTION

Total Community Action, Inc. has been a leading advocate in the fight against poverty in Louisiana. All of our programs and initiatives, from Head Start and Families Matter to our Home Weatherization and Energy Assistance programs, work toward the goal of educating and empowering individuals and families and enabling them to save, build assets, and move out of poverty.

TCA would like to thank the Department of Health and Human Services and the Office of Children, Youth, and Families for their part in the making of this video and for their unwavering efforts to serve the community.

Dr. Peter Dangerfield
Executive Director

Staff Team
Regina S. Martin, VITA Coordinator
Harvey R. H. Britton, Consultant
James Kelley Terry, Consultant

TCA, Inc. Board of Directors
Mr. James M. Singleton, Sr., President
Mrs. Ellenese Brooks-Simms, Vice President
Ms. Lisa Burns, Secretary
Reverend Charles Southall, III, Chaplain
Honorable Ann Duplessis, State Senator
Honorable Edwin R. Murray, State Senator
Honorable Cheryl Gray, State Representative
Honorable Arthur Morrell, State Representative
Honorable Oliver M. Thomas, City Council Member-at-large
Mrs. Sandra A. Berry
Mr. Gerald V. Williams
Mr. Johnny Jackson, Jr.
Ms. Danielle Johnson-Young
Mr. Charles Rice

Ms. Coral W. Robinson
Ms. Mildred Rockett

Special Thanks
Pearlie H. Elloie, Director, Office of Children, Youth, and Families
Fay J. Wooten, Director of Administration
Cheryl W. Floyd, Comptroller

Special thanks to our Survey Team

Yvonne Alexander, Survey Team Supervisor

Team Members:
Carolyn Johnson
Joann Hebrard
Roylene Baptiste
Florence Hayes
Pandural Pete
Monica Johnson
Cathy Bell
Jacquelyn Williams
Yolanda Berry
Shelita De Rouen
Dianne Brewster
Shelia Warren
Albertha Sanders
Debra Robicheaux
Iris Ferara
Cheryl Randall
Mary Shelby
Dianell Thomas
Margaret Craig
Shannon Lewis

978-0-595-40064-5
0-595-40064-7